JEAN RHYS

A Study of the Short Fiction

A Selection of Titles from Twayne's Studies in Short Fiction Series

Twayne publishes studies of all major short-story writers worldwide. For a complete list contact the Publisher directly.

Twayne's Studies in Short Fiction

Gordon Weaver, General Editor
Oklahoma State University

Jean Rhys. *Reproduced by permission of Penguin Books Ltd.*

JEAN RHYS

A Study of the Short Fiction

Cheryl Alexander Malcolm
David Malcolm

TWAYNE PUBLISHERS
An Imprint of Simon & Schuster Macmillan
New York

PRENTICE HALL INTERNATIONAL
London   Mexico City   New Delhi   Singapore   Sydney   Toronto

ÍNDEX

M LA

HUMCA

Twayne's Studies in Short Fiction Series, No. 61

Copyright © 1996 by Twayne Publishers

Twayne Publishers
An Imprint of Simon & Schuster Macmillan
866 Third Avenue
New York, New York 10022

Library of Congress Cataloging-in-Publication Data

Malcolm, Cheryl Alexander.
    Jean Rhys : a study of the short fiction / Cheryl Alexander Malcolm and David Malcolm.
        p.   cm.—(Twayne's studies in short fiction ; no. 61)
    Includes bibliographical references (p.   ) and index.
    ISBN 0-8057-0855-3 (cloth : alk. paper)
    1. Rhys, Jean—Criticism and interpretation.   2. Women and literature—England—History—20th century.   3. Short story.   I. Malcolm, David, 1952–   II. Title.   III. Series.
PR6035.H96Z79   1995
823'.912—dc20   95-30612
                                                                             CIP

The paper used in this publication meets the minimum requirements of the American National Standard for Information Sciences—Permanence of Paper for Printed Library Materials, ANSI Z39.48–1984. ⊗ ™

10 9 8 7 6 5 4 3 2 1

Printed in the United States of America

to our parents
Despina and Christopher Alexander
and
Helen and William Malcolm

Contents

Contents

Preface

In a way that could only have pleased her, Jean Rhys keeps some pretty fast critical company these days. Over the last decade there has been a proliferation of books and articles about her fiction and a lengthy critical biography; two of her novels have been filmed; and the stream of work addressing the author's strikingly slim fictional output—five short novels, three volumes of short stories, and a small number of other brief pieces—shows little sign of abating. Coral Howells's excellent recent study, in which she makes a very convincing case for seeing Rhys as a major feminist, colonial, and modernist voice in twentieth-century fiction, is typical in this respect.[1] Gayatri Chakravorty Spivak sees Rhys as a central figure in her essay on "Three Women's Texts and a Critique of Imperialism."[2] V. S. Naipaul treats her with great respect as an exiled Caribbean writer,[3] and in Lorna Sage's *Women in the House of Fiction: Post-War Women Novelists*, Rhys is there ("up there," as they say) with Simone de Beauvoir, Doris Lessing, Nathalie Sarraute, Iris Murdoch, and Toni Morrison.[4] The literary critical world seems to be trying to make amends for a life of disappointment, indigence, and leaky roofs.

In the decade after her death, Rhys's critical moment has come. In some ways this is scarcely surprising, although few could have predicted this as recently as the 1960s. The U.S. critical and teaching worlds, in particular, find Rhys a particularly congenial figure. Her own partially marginalized existence, her West Indian origin, her Bohemian life-style, her range of experiences (how many major British writers have gone to jail, however briefly?) make her a fascinating figure suitable for a socially critical academic establishment. And her writing itself, focusing as it does upon male exploitation of women, on women's resistance to and collusion with that exploitation, on marginalized, exiled figures from the Third World, on class antagonisms and conflicts, makes her a figure much in tune with contemporary critical concerns in the Anglo-U.S. academy. Rhys's position too as a contemporary and acquaintance of Hemingway and Ford means that she can be seen as an exemplary female modernist voice by, for example, Mary Lou Emery and Veronica Marie Gregg.[5] Jean Rhys herself might say that it has all come a bit late, but it is a restitution of sorts.[6] Her reputation and her position within the evolving canon of major contemporary literature can only become more secure.

Perhaps inevitably and rightly, it is the novels which have received the lion's share of critical attention. They are without doubt Rhys's most complex and sustained achievements, and in *Voyage in the Dark* and *Wide Sargasso Sea*, she wrote two of the most condensed and yet lucid, the most passionate yet technically controlled twentieth-century British novels. Her achievement may be slim, but it is enormous. The short stories, however, have, on the whole, been rather neglected by critics. Rhys's own hesitations and reticences about her short fiction are symptomatic of a certain lack of critical attention. Carole Angier's biography of Rhys is typical (and probably justified) here in the way it declares that lack of space makes it impossible to treat the short stories adequately (Angier, xi). But other studies and essays too tend to focus exclusively on the novels. There are exceptions to this, and these are noted in the bibliography of this book. It is interesting to note, however, that besides older studies, such as those of Staley and Davidson, and articles such as that by A. C. Morrell, both Howells and Sage in their recent and critically very up-to-the-moment books pay considerable attention to the short fiction.[7] Once again, one can predict that Rhys's reputation as a short-story writer can only increase, and her stories find a wider and approving audience, particularly in U.S. colleges and universities. Her position as a marginalized woman writer from a complex colonial background and her concern with gender-related, colonial, and racial topics are sure to arouse considerable interest in U.S. educational institutions in the 1990s.

For all the critical references to Jean Rhys's technical skill as a writer (implicitly recognized by Ford in his preface to *The Left Bank*) and the well-documented care with which she worked at her novels and short stories, there has been little discussion of technical matters in her fiction (Gregg, 37–40). Accordingly, Part 1 of the following study starts with a chapter focusing on precisely those matters—her complex and resourceful deployment of narration, the distinctive stylistic configuration of her short stories, and the nature of plot, action, and setting in them. We note both a substantial skill and variety in technique over all Rhys's fiction, along with a continuity of concern which runs from *The Left Bank* to *Sleep It Off Lady*.

A. C. Morrell's suggestion that Rhys in some measure wrote the same story forty-six times is well-known (Morrell, 243). While this is a simplification (and our chapter on technique points to substantial variety within similarity), it does point to a continuity of concern in much of Rhys's short fiction. Our discussion of individual stories reflects this concern in its central focus on the outsider. A wide range of critics have commented on the centrality of the outsider, largely the marginalized and excluded female figure, in Rhys's writing as a whole. From Ford's preface to A. Alvarez's laudatory appreciation, from reviews of *Tigers Are Better-Looking* to recent academic studies by Molly Hite or Judith Kegan Gardiner, Rhys's concern with the underdog, the normally silenced, the excluded, the ignored is seen to be at the heart of her fiction.[8] Indeed V. S. Naipaul argues that it is precisely the experience of being an outsider rendered in her fiction that makes her writing speak so directly to contemporary readers (Naipaul, 31). To a considerable degree, Rhys's short fiction does not develop substantially over her career. The framework of concerns (and technique), despite some shifts of focus, is laid down in *The Left Bank* and is still there in *Sleep It Off Lady*. It is this overarching concern with the outsider which our discussions of individual stories attempt to establish.

However, our discussions do fall into three main groups which partially reflect the chronology of Rhys's output. The chapters on the three stories from *The Left Bank*, "Illusion," "Mannequin," and "La Grosse Fifi," set out the centrality of the outsider figure in Rhys's short stories and also the complexity with which she deals with such figures and their possibilities for escaping a crushing social and sexual alienation. Four of the following essays largely on stories from *Tigers Are Better-Looking*, "Till September Petronella," "Let Them Call It Jazz" and "Outside the Machine," "A Solid House," and "I Spy A Stranger," show a shift in focus toward specifically English forms of exclusion and marginalization, especially in terms of social class and national-racial identity. Here our arguments take issue with those of, for example, Linda Bamber and Gloria Fromm, who see Rhys as dealing with the outsider in rather vague, highly generalized, ahistorical, and asocial ways.[9] In the remaining three essays, on "The Day They Burned the Books" (from *Tigers Are Better-Looking*), "Pioneers, Oh, Pioneers," and "On Not Shooting Sitting Birds" (from *Sleep It Off Lady*), the focus of our discussions is on the presentation of specifically colonial issues. It must be stressed however that this does not imply a chronological shift in concerns in Rhys's short fiction. Colonial issues are present in *The Left Bank* in the importantly placed "Trio," "Mixing Cocktails," and "Again the Antilles"; a focus on the crushing nature of English social and sexual exclusions is present in the first story from *The Left Bank*,

"Illusion." "Let Them Call It Jazz" is not just about English racial cruelty, but specifically about how that affects a colonized subject. "Sleep It Off Lady" reflects the focus on English attitudes toward marginalized women that is central to "Till September Petronella" and to the long-suppressed stories "I Spy a Stranger" and "Temps Perdi."

The selection of stories to be discussed is admittedly that—a selection. We have tried to combine a thorough treatment of individual texts with an attempt to give an overall sense of Rhys's achievement in her short fiction. Some texts have been excluded because there exist fairly extensive treatments of them in other critical studies (for example, "Tigers Are Better-Looking" or "Good-bye Marcus, Good-bye Rose").[10] The emphasis of our chapters falls firmly on *The Left Bank* and on *Tigers Are Better-Looking*. This is because it seems to us that in these volumes and in the suppressed "I Spy a Stranger," Rhys is operating at her best and most complex. *The Left Bank* stories are no mere juvenilia and apprentice work, but skilled and sophisticated pieces of great interest written by a woman already in her thirties. The stories in *Tigers Are Better-Looking* are the work of a mature writer done over many years (although the volume dates from the 1960s, several stories were written much earlier). Rhys herself tended to be dismissive of the stories in *Sleep It Off Lady*, describing them to David Plante as mere "magazine stories."[11] Indeed this is true at least in part, and although "Pioneers, Oh, Pioneers," "Fishy Waters," "On Not Shooting Sitting Birds," "The Insect World," and "I Used to Live Here Once" are as successful and subtle as anything she wrote, several others show a marked falling off, including the schematic and predictable title story. Rhys's other short fiction, those pieces collected in *My Day*, for example, seem slight in comparison with her earlier work. But it must be emphasized that at her best in *The Left Bank* and in *Tigers Are Better-Looking*, Rhys wrote some very good short stories that in their rigorous exposure of social cruelty, in their economy and subtlety of technique can stand beside her best novels. Indeed, in "La Grosse Fifi," "Till September Petronella," and "I Spy a Stranger" she wrote some of the best short stories in English.[12] In "Let Them Call It Jazz," she went one better; she created a masterpiece.

The authoritative edition (despite a large number of typographical errors) of Rhys's short stories, containing almost every piece of short fiction she published, is *The Collected Short Stories*, edited by Diana Athill and published by Norton in the United States. Although it contains the revised versions of stories from *The Left Bank* that were reprinted in *Tigers Are Better-Looking*, in almost all cases the changes Rhys made for the later collection are minor. All references to individual stories are to the texts printed in this volume. When we have chosen to make references to Rhys's novels, it seemed more reasonable to make these to inexpensive and widely available U.S. and British paperback editions, published by Norton and by Penguin.

Notes

1. Coral Ann Howells, *Jean Rhys* (New York: St. Martin's Press, 1991), 5–6, 11–13—hereafter cited in text.

2. Gayatri Chakravorty Spivak, "Three Women's Texts and a Critique of Imperialism," *Critical Inquiry* 12 (Spring 1985): 243–61 (249–53).

3. V. S. Naipaul, "Without a Dog's Chance," Review of *After Leaving Mr. Mackenzie* by Jean Rhys, *New York Review of Books*, 18 May 1972, 29–31—hereafter cited in text.

4. Lorna Sage, *Women in the House of Fiction: Post-War Women Novelists* (New York: Routledge, 1992), 47–54—hereafter cited in text.

5. Mary Lou Emery, *Jean Rhys at "World's End": Novels of Colonial and Social Exile* (Austin: University of Texas Press, 1990), x, 4–32—hereafter cited in text. Veronica Marie Gregg, "Jean Rhys and Modernism: A Different Voice," *Jean Rhys Review* 1 (Spring 1987): 30–46—hereafter cited in text.

6. Carole Angier, *Jean Rhys: Life and Work* (Boston, Toronto, London: Little, Brown, and Co., 1990), 606—hereafter cited in text.

7. Thomas F. Staley, *Jean Rhys: A Critical Study* (Austin: University of Texas Press, 1979), 20–34, 121–31; Arnold E. Davidson, *Jean Rhys* (New York; Frederick Ungar, 1985), 113–33; A. C. Morrell, "The World of Jean Rhys's Short Stories," *World Literature Written in English* 18, no. 1 (April 1979): 235–44—hereafter cited in text. See also: Howells, 29–43, 124–46; and Sage, 48–50, 52–4.

8. A. Alvarez, "The Best Living English Novelist," *New York Times Book Review*, 17 March 1974, 6–7 (7); Mary Sullivan, "All Underdogs," Review of *Tigers Are Better-Looking* by Jean Rhys, *Listener*, 25 April 1968, 549; Molly Hite, *The Other Side of the Story: Structures and Strategies of Contemporary Feminist Narrative* (Ithaca and London: Cornell University Press, 1989), 25, 47—hereafter cited in text; Judith Kegan Gardiner, *Rhys, Stead, Lessing, and the Politics of Empathy* (Bloomington and Indianapolis: Indiana University Press, 1989), 24—hereafter cited in text.

9. Linda Bamber, "Jean Rhys," *Partisan Review* 49 (1982): 92–100; Gloria Fromm, "Making up Jean Rhys," *New Criterion*, December 1985, 47–50.

10. See, for example: Morrell 237–8 and Howells 129–32, 135–8.

11. David Plante, *Difficult Women: A Memoir of Three* (London: Victor Gollancz, 1983), 38—hereafter cited in text.

12. Gardiner puts her in the company of Joyce, Mansfield, and Tillie Olsen (19).

Acknowledgments

Excerpts from *Jean Rhys: The Collected Short Stories*, published by W. W. Norton and Company, Inc., in 1987, are reproduced by permission of the Wallace Literary Agency, Inc. Copyright © 1960, 1962, 1963, 1966, 1967, 1976 by Jean Rhys. "Illusion," "From a French Prison," "In a Café," "Tout Montparnasse and a Lady," "Mannequin," "Tea with an Artist," "Trio," "Mixing Cocktails," "Hunger," "A Night," "Learning to Be a Mother," "At the Villa d'Or," "La Grosse Fifi," and "Vienne" are from *The Left Bank* and were first published by Jonathan Cape (London) and Harper and Brothers (New York) in 1927. "Till September Petronella," "Let Them Call It Jazz," "Outside the Machine," "The Lotus," "A Solid House," and "The Day They Burned the Books," are from *Tigers Are Better-Looking*, which was first published in 1968 by André Deutsch (London) and by Harper & Row (New York) in 1974. "I Spy a Stranger" was first published in *Penguin Modern Stories* (London). "Pioneers, Oh, Pioneers," "Fishy Waters," "The Insect World," "On Not Shooting Sitting Birds," and "Sleep It Off Lady" are from *Sleep It Off Lady*, which was first published in 1976 by Harper & Row (New York).

Excerpts from the above short stories are also reproduced by permission of Penguin Books Ltd.

From Jean Rhys, *Voyage in the Dark*. Copyright © 1934 by Jean Rhys. Reproduced by permission of Penguin Books Ltd. and W. W. Norton and Company, Inc.

From Jean Rhys, *Wide Sargasso Sea*. Copyright © 1966 by Jean Rhys. Reproduced by permission of Penguin Books Ltd. and W. W. Norton and Company, Inc.

From *The Letters of Jean Rhys*. Selection © Francis Wyndham and Diana Melly, 1984. Introduction copyright © Francis Wyndham, 1984. Letters copyright © the Estate of Jean Rhys, 1984. Reproduced by permission of Sheil Land Associates Limited and by permission of Penguin Books Ltd.

From David Plante, *Difficult Women: A Memoir of Three*. Reproduced by permission of Aiken, Stone and Wylie Limited.

Acknowledgments

From "Stories Reduced to Essentials: Jean Rhys a Remarkable New Hand Disdains to Squander Any Phrases on Atmosphere" by Conrad Aiken. Originally appeared in the *New York Evening Post*. Copyright 1927 by Conrad Aiken. Reprinted by permission of Brandt and Brandt Literary Agents, Inc.

From Review of *The Left Bank and Other Stories*, *New Statesman*, 30 April 1927. Copyright New Statesman and Society. Reproduced with kind permission of New Statesman and Society.

From Review of *The Left Bank and Other Stories*, *Times Literary Supplement*, 5 May 1927. First published in the *Times Literary Supplement*. Reproduced by permission of the *Times Literary Supplement*.

From Ford Madox Ford, "Preface: Rive Gauche," *The Left Bank and Other Stories* by Jean Rhys. Used by permission of Janice Biala.

From Francis Hope, "Did You Once See Paris Plain?" Review of *Tigers Are Better-Looking*, *Observer*, 31 March 1968. Francis Hope The Observer ©. Published by permission of The Observer ©.

From Review of *Tigers Are Better-Looking*. Reprinted from the 26 August 1974 issue of *Publishers Weekly*, published by R. R. Bowker Company, a Xerox company. Copyright © 1974 by Xerox Corporation.

From Diane Johnson, "Overdrawn at the Left Bank of the World," Review of *Tigers Are Better-Looking*, *Washington Post Book World*, 3 November 1974. © 1974 The Washington Post. Reprinted with permission.

From Robert Leiter, Review of *Tigers Are Better-Looking*, *New Republic*, 7 December 1974. Reprinted by permission of *The New Republic*, © 1974, The New Republic, Inc.

From George Stade, "A Spark, an Amis, a Rhys," Review of *Tigers Are Better-Looking*, *New York Times Book Review*, 20 October 1974. Copyright © 1974 by The New York Times Company. Reprinted by permission.

From Susannah Clapp, "Bleak Treats," Review of *Sleep It Off, Lady*, *New Statesman*, 22 October 1976. Copyright New Statesman and Society. Reproduced with kind permission of New Statesman and Society.

From Nick Totton, "Speak Memory," Review of *Sleep It Off, Lady*, *Spectator*, 30 October 1976. Reproduced by permission of The Spectator.

From Rayner Heppenstall, "Bitter-sweet," Review of *Tigers Are Better-Looking*, *Spectator*, 5 April 1968. Reproduced by permission of The Spectator.

From Paul Piazza, "The World of Jean Rhys," *Chronicle of Higher Education*, 7 March 1977. Reprinted by permission of Paul Piazza. From Molly Hite, *The Other Side of the Story: Structures and Strategies of Contemporary Feminist Narrative*. Copyright © 1989 by Cornell University Press. Used by permission of the publisher, Cornell University Press.

From Veronica Marie Gregg, "Jean Rhys and Modernism: A Different Voice," *Jean Rhys Review* 1 (Spring 1987). Reproduced by permission of the Jean Rhys Review.

From Laura Niesen de Abruna, "Jean Rhys's Feminism: Theory against Practice," *World Literature Written in English* 28, no. 2 (1988). Reprinted by permission of *World Literature Written in English*.

From Linda Bamber, "Jean Rhys," *Partisan Review* 49 (1982). Reproduced by permission of Linda Bamber.

From Nancy J. Leigh, "Mirror, Mirror: The Development of Female Identity in Jean Rhys's Fiction," *World Literature Written in English* 25, no. 2 (1985). Reprinted by permission of *World Literature Written in English*.

From Coral Ann Howells, *Jean Rhys*. First published by Harvester Wheatsheaf, Hemel Hempstead, UK (1991). Reproduced by permission of Harvester Wheatsheaf. Copyright © 1991 St. Martin's Press. Reprinted with permission of St. Martin's Press, Incorporated.

We would also like to thank our editor, Pauline Sultana, and our copy editor, Brenda Goldberg, for their helpful suggestions during the final developmental stages of this volume.

Part 1

THE SHORT FICTION

Jean Rhys's Art of the Short Story

Narrators and Narration

One of the most striking aspects of narration in Rhys's short fiction is the variety of narrational devices that it employs. Rhys uses both female and nongendered narrators; the narrational tone ranges from the ironic ("Tout Montparnasse") to the detached ("Kismet") to the passionately engaged ("Let Them Call It Jazz" and "Temps Perdi"). She adopts subjective and objective points of view and deploys participant and nonparticipant narrators throughout her short fiction; she combines the techniques of narrated action with dialogue and free direct and indirect speech. Taken as a whole, her stories display a remarkable resourcefulness in narration.

In *The Left Bank*, half the stories (eleven of twenty-two) are specifically narrated by women. In some, for example in "Vienne," this is very obvious; in others, for example in "Illusion" and "Tea with an Artist," the narrator's gender is almost casually indicated in dialogue (and is perhaps all the more important because of its understated presence). In the other stories, the narrator is genderless, although the predominant point of view is frequently that of a woman character, for example, in "At the Villa d'Or" and "La Grosse Fifi." Only occasionally does Rhys adopt a male point of view—in "In the Luxembourg Gardens" and "The Grey Day" (although in both this is combined with an ironic tone and a satirical purpose), and in the grim "The Sidi." There are, however, minor shifts to a male point of view in "At the Villa d'Or" (Mr. Valentine) and "La Grosse Fifi" (Mark).

Rhys employs participant and nonparticipant narrators equally (11/11), and moves through a range of narrational technique with skill and ease. Her narrators are never truly omniscient, and even when they seem so, she attempts to qualify their knowledge. For example, in "From a French Prison" we learn of the prisoner that "the quarter of an hour would seem terribly short to him and always he listened for the shout of the warder to summon him away and always he feared not being on the alert to answer it" (12). The narration also hovers

3

between complete knowledge and external observation with the old man at the end. "His mouth drooped, his huge brown eyes stared solemnly at an incomprehensible world" (12). The only examples of omniscience occur in those minor shifts to a male point of view in "At the Villa d'Or" and "La Grosse Fifi." A favored technique in *The Left Bank* is, however, that of limited omniscience—the point of view in "Tout Montparnasse" and "Mannequin." Rhys occasionally transmits this point of view through free indirect speech or thought, where the third-person text begins to take on the rhythms and words of the character. She does this, for example, with the American protagonist of "Tout Montparnasse," with Anna in "Mannequin," and in its most radical form with Roseau in "La Grosse Fifi."

> In other words: you won't be rotten—now. Will you, will you? I'll do anything you like, but be kind to me, won't you, won't you?
> Not that it didn't sound better in French.
> "Now," read Fifi, "I can walk lightly for I have laid my life in the hands of my lover.
> "Change, change ma vie, aux mains de mon amant!" And so on, and so on.
> Roseau thought that it was horrible to hear this ruin of a woman voicing all her own moods, all her own thoughts. Horrible. (87)

But Rhys also often adopts a detached observer's point of view, both with a participant narrator, as in "Illusion," or with a nonparticipant one, as in "From a French Prison" and "In a Café." "Mannequin" moves subtly between Anna's point of view and a detached perspective.

> At six o'clock Anna was out in the rue de la Paix; her fatigue forgotten, the feeling that now she really belonged to the great, maddening city possessed her and she was happy in her beautifully cut tailor-made and beret.
> Georgette passed her and smiled; Babette was in a fur coat.
> All up the street the mannequins were coming out of the shops, pausing on the pavements a moment, making them as gay and as beautiful as beds of flowers before they walked swiftly away and the Paris night swallowed them up. (25–6)

At times, the narrator effaces himself/herself, and the text has dramatic aspects. Examples of this include the framed narratives of "A Spiritualist" and "The Blue Bird," and also the monologues of "Hunger" and "A Night," and the peculiar, one-sided "Discourse of a Lady." In his preface to *The Left Bank*, Ford indicates that the author will be, as it were, a guide to the Bohemia of the stories' settings.[1] The narrators of many of the stories, both participant and nonparticipant, clearly fill this role. They are usually, in a certain sense, knowledgeable narrators, privy to some kinds of special information. The narrator of "Illusion" can tell us of Miss Bruce that she "had, of course, like most of the English and American artists in Paris, a private income— a respectably large one, I believe" (2). The narrator is also able to speculate in a seemingly authoritative fashion on Miss Bruce's state of mind while buying one of her many beautiful dresses. "Miss Bruce had seen a dress and suddenly thought: in that dress perhaps. . . . And, immediately afterwards: why not? And had entered the shop, and, blushing slightly, had asked the price. That had been the first time: an accident, an impulse" (4). (Of course, like so much else in this story, the knowledge is an illusion. The narrator does not know Miss Bruce at all. Here she is passing speculation or, indeed, self-revelation off as knowledge.) The narrator of "From a French Prison" knows all the details of prison visiting. "At the gate of the prison all the permits must be given up . . ." (12). The narrator of "In a Café" is our experienced guide to this demimonde, at one point briefly explaining what "the *grues*" referred to in the song are. The narrators of "Tout Montparnasse," "Tea with an Artist," "In the Rue de l'Arriveé," "The Blue Bird," and "The Sidi" exhibit a similar knowledgeability about Paris and the world of the Left Bank which they are willing to impart to us from a position of authority.

But this knowledge is strictly limited to external factors, to social mores, or to the accepted meaning of words. It stands in sharp contrast to the actual ignorance of others, their motives and impulses, which mark so many narrators and characters in Rhys's fiction. Indeed, many of the narrators are strikingly unknowing at times. Certainly, the secondary, male narrator of "A Spiritualist" has no idea of his guilt and the shabbiness of his behavior toward his mistress, but one does wonder why the narrator of "From a French Prison" knows so much, or indeed anything, about such a milieu. What is he/she not telling us about his/her reasons for being there? Indeed, the seemingly rather detached narrators of "Illusion" and "Tea with an Artist" pretend to have rather too much knowledge of their subjects, Miss Bruce, Verhausen, and Marthe, more than can possibly be justified in the stories. Are they

Part 1

not rather talking about themselves, their own fates and characters in ways that they dare not acknowledge openly? They seem to be obliquely and unknowingly presenting their own predicaments through an assumed knowledge of others.

The Left Bank as a whole shows a shift in narrational stance from that of objective observer of externals to a much greater subjectivity both in third- and first-person narratives. The pattern in the collection is quite clear. In the first eight stories—"Illusion" through "Tea with an Artist"—the narrator is fundamentally an observer of physical externals. The only substantial exception is the satirical passage of free indirect thought in "Tout Montparnasse." Even "Mannequin" places a strong emphasis on the externally observable, while the secondary narrator of "A Spiritualist" is marked by his inability to explore feelings. The next six stories, however—"Trio" through "A Night"—involve first-person narrators who are, to say the least, much more interested in exploring their feelings and psychological states. Even "Again the Antilles" ends on an intensely personal note, and the whole story can be seen as an affectionate reminiscence exposing a sense of loss. Of the remaining stories, "In the Rue de l'Arriveé," "The Grey Day," "The Sidi," "At the Villa d'Or," and "La Grosse Fifi" recount events from a particular point of view with all its emotional and psychological attitudes. Even the framed "The Blue Bird" has an emotional self-exposure at its heart. This subjective element is most evident in "La Grosse Fifi," in which Roseau's responses to events are given in a very direct form. "Learning to Be a Mother" and "Vienne" are highly subjective pieces, concerned above all with presenting particular psychological and emotional experiences.

In this configuration of stories, it is very striking that a subjective stance, be it first- or third-person, emerges with the brief "Trio," in which the narrator describes in some detail the appearance of three black West Indians in Paris. The story ends, however, on an unexpected and highly personal note: "It was because these were my compatriots that in that Montparnasse restaurant I remembered the Antilles" (35). There follow several intensely subjective pieces such as "Hunger" and "A Night," and the collection never returns to the laconic detachment of "Illusion" or "From a French Prison." In the collection as a whole, the first West Indian story and the two that follow it form a crucial hinge and provide support for those critics who see Rhys's West Indian origins and concerns as central to her output.

6

* * *

The same resourcefulness and variety in narration can be seen in Rhys's later stories. *Tigers Are Better-Looking, Sleep It Off Lady* and the wartime pair, "I Spy a Stranger" and "Temps Perdi" exhibit a wide variety of narrators and narrational techniques. A number of texts stand out as particularly resourceful in terms of their narration—"A Solid House," with its extensive use of free indirect speech; the quasi-dramatic "The Sound of the River" "I Spy a Stranger," with its mixture of dialogue, reported narration, and document; and "Fishy Waters," in which a sordid criminal case is recounted through letters, a newspaper report, and a third-person, point-of-view narration. The range of points of view in terms of age and gender, and of race and social class ("Let Them Call It Jazz"), is also quite considerable. Indeed, *Sleep It Off Lady* aims at a generality of focus in its movement from childhood narration and point of view to those of old age and death.

In *Sleep It Off Lady*, two other patterns emerge with regard to narration. First, the oblique narrational position that we noted in *The Left Bank* recurs. In a number of stories, narrators seem to be unknowingly speaking about themselves through others' predicaments. This is the case in "Before the Deluge," "Rapunzel," and perhaps in "Kismet." In these, the narrators' very reticence about themselves suggests that their own fates somehow parallel those of the characters they depict. Second, the act of memory is foregrounded in connection with a number of narrators in this collection. Many stories are explicitly presented as acts of recollection of distant events—"The Bishop's Feast," "Heat," and "On Not Shooting Sitting Birds." This is also true of the uncollected stories "The Whistling Bird" and "Invitation to the Dance." "I Used to Live Here Once" can also be seen as belonging to this grouping, with the *revenante* representing other narrators' returns to long-lost places, only to find themselves cut off from such places by time and mortality.

Style

Critics have commented extensively on Jean Rhys's style and frequently noted its distinctiveness.[2] Rhys's own care as a stylist is well documented in letters and in recorded conversations.[3] However, little attempt has been made to analyze the elements of the Rhys style. Clearly this style is not uniform; a writing career spanning some fifty years and an output of over twenty short stories would make that unlikely. But certain recurrent stylistic tendencies are observable across Rhys's work as a whole.

The features are clear in *The Left Bank*. Although sentence length and type vary considerably in the collection as a whole, there are numerous passages that are marked by Rhys's use of short and simple or compound sentences. For example, the opening three paragraphs of "Trio" contain only one complex sentence (the first) (34). This is equally evident in the opening of "Hunger," where again the first three paragraphs show only one complex sentence (the fourth) (42). The opening of "Vienne" prunes syntax even further, and elliptical statements and fragments predominate among the very short paragraphs.

> Funny how it's slipped away, Vienna. Nothing left but a few snapshots.
> Not a friend, not a pretty frock—nothing left of Vienna.
> Hot sun, my black frock, a hat with roses, music, lots of music—
> The little dancer at the Parisien with a Kirchner girl's legs and a little faun's face. (94)

Indeed, short paragraphs are another marked stylistic feature of these stories. The single-sentence paragraph or fragment paragraph abound. This is very evident in "A Night," but one can see it too, for example, in the conclusion of "Learning to Be a Mother" (58–9). Even in this passage, which contains three complex sentences, any sense of stylistic elevation is countered by the shortness of the paragraphs and the relative simplicity of the vocabulary. In this last respect, the passage is further representative of Rhys's style. Her vocabulary is, except in one striking way, consistently simple and accessible. Vocabulary is usually neither very elevated nor formal nor abstruse. The only substantial exception is in the author's use of French vocabulary and syntax in several stories. This is very marked in a number of texts—"Illusion," "A Spiritualist," "Mannequin," "Learning to Be a Mother," and "La Grosse Fifi." For example, in "Learning to Be a Mother," " '*Regardez*,' says Mme. Laboriau, '*comme il est beau votre fils*. . . .' Look how beautiful is your son!" (56). In "Vienne," French vocabulary and syntax are coupled with (sometimes rather inaccurate) German to give the polyglot atmosphere of Vienna, Budapest, and the rest of its Central European setting (101).

Not only is the English of many stories subject to foreign influence, but the narrators and characters themselves often have their utterances penetrated and shaped by others' text. "Le Saut dans l'Inconnu" is an inescapable, repeated, remembered tag in "A Night," which also ends with a litany to the Virgin (47–9). Miss Dufreyne in "In the Rue de l'Arriveé" is cast down by the text she reads in a sordid pharmacy window and made slightly happier by the poor passerby's words of sympathy. In "Learning to Be a Mother," the narrator rebels against and then conforms to the concept of "La Femme Sacreé," while both Fifi and Roseau seem to be paralyzed and trapped by the melancholy charms of the French verse they read ("La Grosse Fifi").

Although certain stylistic tendencies are clear, Rhys's style in *The Left Bank* is by no means uniform. Several stories show a much more complex and formal style. For example, the protagonists of "Tout Montparnasse" are introduced through complex sentences and sophisticated vocabulary, while in "Tea with an Artist" the narrator describes the surroundings of Verhausen's studio in a rather elevated style [a policeman has an expression of "contemplative stupefaction," a dog "lay stretched philosophically," and the narrator "toiled" up the stairs (30)]. A similar formality of vocabulary and syntax can be seen in the second paragraph of "In the Rue de l'Arriveé," or at certain points of "At the Villa d'Or." These passages, however, are limited in number when set against the stories' normally accessible vocabulary and pruned syntax. Indeed, formal and elevated passages often mark a limited perspective which is undermined by the rest of the story. The "romantic" American lady artist in "Tout Montparnasse" is wholly mistaken about the young man she observes. The linguistic confidence and detachment of the narrator in "Tea with an Artist" is shattered by the figure of Marthe, while the narrator indicates in her laconic "Poor Sara . . . also a Romantic" that the elevated syntax and vocabulary at the Villa d'Or may mask an unhappy outcome to Sara's stay there.

The stylistic configuration of Rhys's stories is well established by *The Left Bank*: a simplicity of vocabulary and syntax, a pruning of style to the fragment and the very short (often one-line) paragraph, a marked foreign influence on vocabulary and syntax, and a permeation of narrators' and characters' discourse by others' texts and utterances. The functions of stylistic elements are always very difficult to establish, but one might suggest that these features of Rhys's style above all aim at an accessibility. The simple vocabulary, the rarely very complex sentence structure, the telegramlike paragraphs certainly make the stories relatively easy to read. But these stylistic elements have other functions.

They often give a sense of intense subjectivity in keeping with the focus of the texts. These short paragraphs and fragmented utterances convincingly suggest the emotional responses and impressions of narrators and characters. After all, these are not formal presentations to others, but the private and inward movements of the soul. Perhaps too they suggest a weariness, a weakness, a lack of stamina, which would accord well with the victimized and damaged figures of Rhys's stories. The occasional permeation of a character's or narrator's speech by the text of another would also illustrate this function, while the very foreignness of so much of these Rhys short stories would fit in well with the alienation from and questioning of Anglo-Saxon hypocrisies and brutalities that inform so many of her stories (and novels).

As with narration and point of view, Rhys's later stories follow the stylistic pattern laid down in *The Left Bank*. Vocabulary and syntax remain accessible; even where sentences are technically complex, they are rarely long, nor is their vocabulary complex. The opening two paragraphs of "Till September Petronella" illustrate this well (125). Despite the presence of a number of complex sentences here, the impression is finally not different from that of most stories in *The Left Bank*. Any sense of elevation is undercut by the informality of the vocabulary ("A bit of a change"), by contractions ("doesn't," "wasn't"), by the prominence of coordinating conjunctions, by the vagueness of reference of "them" in paragraph 2, and by the tense shift that immediately follows, so typical of informal narration ("and you stand there"). The same kind of accessible, pruned style we saw in *The Left Bank* recurs throughout the rest of the short fiction. "The Insect World" provides some representative passages [see, for example, "In front of her stood an elderly woman . . ." (356)].

In addition, the penetration of narrators' and characters' texts by those of others is very marked in stories after those of *The Left Bank*. "Fishy Waters," for example, is explicitly about the power of others' texts over the mind of Maggie Penrice. In "The Insect World," Audrey's enjoyment of her book is poisoned by the marginal notes of a previous male reader, she is bullied into buying a dress she does not want, and a half-remembered quotation haunts her as she lies awake. In an interesting reciprocal action, Laura's words permeate Mrs. Hudson's and Mrs. Trant's conversation, but are also imprisoned within it ("I Spy a Stranger"). Petronella, her mind filled with "long romantic novels" (125), with the banal urgings of others [" '*Look gay*,' they say" (131)], with memories of others' dialogue [" '*You have it*,' *he said. The other one said, 'Want a lift?'* " (145)], and with the line that paradoxically she could never say on stage is representative of this aspect of Rhys's stories. In this respect she is similar to Miss Verney in "Sleep It Off Lady," who constantly recalls and quotes others' texts ("after many a summer dies the swan, as some man said" (375).

Tigers Are Better-Looking contains one unique and striking stylistic experiment, "Let Them Call It Jazz." Written in an attempt at black West Indian dialect, an attempt about which Rhys was at times concerned,[4] it stands out among the other stories and gives the lie to those who charge Rhys with a limited range.[5] It also indicates some of the possibilities she might have had as a writer if life had only been a little kinder to her, and it suggests in stylistic terms how vital the West Indies and her sense of identification with them are to Rhys's writing.

Plot and Action

Rhys's short stories are quite traditional in their ordering of events. Action is always given in linear, chronological order without the narrative experimentation one finds in some twentieth-century story writing by Conrad, Kipling, Faulkner, or Katherine Anne Porter. This linear, chronological element is found even within framed stories such as "A Spiritualist" or "The Blue Bird" and within memory pieces such as "Vienne," "Temps Perdi," and "Pioneers, Oh, Pioneers." These all involve a traditional linear, chronological narrative within a frame (someone tells the narrator a story) or within an act of recall.

The nature of the action itself, however, is in keeping with developments in much modern twentieth-century literature. Plot is usually rudimentary and lacks the complications and exciting events of much traditional short-story writing. The action is often marked by triviality, by its banal and sordid qualities. In many of Rhys's stories, there is no action at all in the traditional literary sense; as in Beckett's *Waiting for Godot*, often nothing happens. Contemporary critics noticed this in reviews of *The Left Bank*, and stories in it are frequently described as vignettes rather than stories proper.[6] This is clearly true of pieces such as "Trio," "Mixing Cocktails," and "At the Villa d'Or," and the monologues "Hunger" and "A Night." But it is also true of later stories such as "A Solid House," parts of "Temps Perdi," and "The Insect World." Action in the traditional sense seems pruned almost to nonexistence.

This reductive tendency is apparent in many of the other stories.

Complexities of plot, exciting crises, complications, and dénouements are almost entirely lacking. Anna starts work in a fashion house; she eats lunch and leaves ("Mannequin"). The narrator visits a reclusive artist and his mistress/wife ("Tea with an Artist"). The narrator has a baby ("Learning to Be a Mother"). A young poet feels sad ("The Grey Day"). Inez recovers from an operation in the hospital ("Outside the Machine"). Audrey has a day off during the War and feels miserable ("The Insect World"). Even in stories in which "more" happens, such as "Till September Petronella" or "A Night Out 1925," the events are scarcely of a dramatic or exciting nature, nor are they organized in a complicated plot. There are obvious exceptions—the brutal events of "The Sidi," the dramatic bankruptcy and flight in "Vienne," the brawling and imprisonment of "Let Them Call It Jazz" and "Tigers Are Better-Looking," and the deaths at the end of "The Sound of the River" and "Sleep It Off Lady." However, at times narrational strategy seems to be designed to undercut any violent or exciting events. The framing and banal ending of "The Blue Bird" do just that; Fifi's violent death is mediated briefly through a newspaper report ("La Grosse Fifi"); and Laura's ostracism and virtual imprisonment is given through Mrs. Hudson's and Mrs. Trant's conversation ("I Spy a Stranger"). We learn of Ramage's madness and suicide through a child's unfocused memories ("Pioneers, Oh, Pioneers") and of the complications of the Longa case through letters and a retelling of a newspaper report ("Fishy Waters"). In some cases the limited nature of a story's action is deliberately set against a global cataclysm offstage—the Great War in "Till September Petronella" and the Second World War in "The Insect World."

Of course, the action may be limited in one sense, in traditional literary terms trivial or sordid or banal, but it is not so in a wider psychological or social sense. Even the stories with the most limited action, the least dramatic events, involve major experiences for the characters and major experiences of a general nature—of emotional and cultural repression ("Illusion"), of sexual conformity ("Mannequin," "Learning to Be a Mother"), of casual male brutality toward women ("Rapunzel, Rapunzel"), of the hazards of social acceptance ("On Not Shooting Sitting Birds"), and of racial conflict and complexity ("The Day They Burned the Books"). Although nothing seems to be happening, a great deal is.

Setting

Space is almost always urban in Rhys's short stories. A room, a café, a city park, a city street—these are her favored settings throughout her fiction. Even when stories do not take place in the city, they have largely interior settings. Rhys's world is usually enclosed and manmade. The heroine of "Vienne" only sees the Central European landscape from her speeding car. For Petronella, the rural world outside the cottage is hostile, and she leaves it for car, pub, train, and club as soon as possible ("Till September Petronella"). The sound of the river is frightening, and in any case it is only a background to the couple's night dialogue ("The Sound of the River").

Rhys's settings are also often exotic and cosmopolitan—the Left Bank of Paris, Central Europe, the West Indies—but are also often local and drab—London during the Second World War, an English provincial town. The stories with a West Indian setting do sometimes look outside the room or the house ("Mixing Cocktails," "Pioneers, Oh, Pioneers"). But only fleetingly and in memory do they form any kind of *locus amoenus*, any kind of benign setting. The natural beauty of Spanish Castle is the site of Ramage's madness and death ("Pioneers, Oh, Pioneers"); in "I Used to Live Here Once," it is in any case gone beyond recall.

In keeping with the enclosed nature of so many of Rhys's settings are the recurrent prison motifs. Her short fiction is full of prisons of one sort or another. There are literal prisons in "From a French Prison," "The Sidi," "Let Them Call It Jazz," "Tigers Are Better-Looking," and "I Spy a Stranger." But there are many settings that are clearly places of confinement in a metaphorical sense—the closet in which Miss Bruce imprisons her bright clothes ("Illusion"), the labyrinthine fashion house that fits Anna to its mold ("Mannequin"), the golden cage of the Villa d'Or ("At the Villa d'Or"), the English hospital and the class power and prejudice it represents ("Outside the Machine"), "Rolveden" in "Temps Perdi," and the constricted, hostile surroundings of Mrs. Verney in "Sleep It Off Lady." Above all, Rhys's settings are places of entrapment—physical, social and sexual—and are part of her vision of the world as a hostile, endlessly cruel, and alienating place which entraps and grinds down her heroines.

Protagonists

Rhys's short fiction shows a considerable range of protagonists and main characters. Much of the criticism focusing on "the Rhys woman" has ignored this. However, not all protagonists are female—see, for example, "Tigers Are Better-Looking" and "Fishy Waters." Also, Rhys's female protagonists vary greatly, above all in age. This is particularly clear in *Sleep It Off Lady*, in which the stories follow a chronological progression from early childhood to old age and death. And in Selina, the black West Indian protagonist of "Let Them Call It Jazz," Rhys focuses on experiences and uses a language until recently largely excluded from British fiction.

Despite differences, however, Rhys's protagonists do show certain similarities, and these will be extensively discussed in the following section of this book, which considers individual stories in detail.

Outsiders/Insiders

"Illusion"—A World of Outsiders

"Illusion," the first story in Rhys's 1927 collection *The Left Bank*, can be said to be about dresses.

> In the middle, hanging in the place of honour, was an evening dress of a very beautiful shade of gold: near it another of flame colour: of two black dresses the one was touched with silver, the other with a jaunty embroidery of emerald and blue. There were a black and white check with a jaunty belt, a flowered *crepe de chine*—positively flowered!—then a carnival costume complete with mask, then a huddle, a positive huddle of all colours, of all stuffs. (3)

The dresses are effectively skeletons in the closet, raising questions about Miss Bruce's "cool sensible, tidy English outside" (2). They are flamboyant and fun; they are un-English. They are, it seems, from another world, one marked by its vivid colors and closely resembling the West Indies remembered by Anna in *Voyage in the Dark*. Anna distinguishes England and the West Indies in terms of colors. "The colours [in the West Indies] are red, purple, blue, gold, all shades of green. The colours here [England] are black, brown, grey, dim-green, pale blue, the white of people's faces—like woodlice."[8]

The excitement that is conveyed in the description of the dresses owes as much to the structure of the sentences as to the actual rendering of images. The passage begins slowly enough with three clauses, each one longer than the next, the last containing no less than six adjectives referring to the word "dress." Then a list of dresses follows, more concisely and vividly described in short phrases broken by dashes and a mid-sentence exclamation mark. A sense of building excitement comes in the repetition of the words "jaunty," "flowered," "huddle," and "all," which serves to connect one image with the next until the syntax nearly breaks down altogether and the speaker seems spent of words to describe what she sees.

The dresses are not merely colorful, they are dramatically colored. The yellows are not pale, like the ineffectual sun in England. In the later story "Let Them Call It Jazz," the West Indian Selina Davis talks of "a glare" without warmth in England (161), while in "Till September Petronella" the English countryside has an oppressive, claustrophobic glare (134–5). Instead, the yellows of Miss Bruce's dresses are "gold" and "flame" colors, comparable in their boldness to the colors of the West Indies, which the male protagonist in *Wide Sargasso Sea* calls "extreme" and "too much,"[9] and to those which the very English Miss Spearman in "A Solid House" is happy not to have on her walls. Instead, she has "pictures of blue sea—but not too blue, not a vulgar tropical blue—of white walls—but not too stark—of shadows—but not too black" (233). Some of Miss Bruce's dresses are un-English by a juxtaposition of colors that creates a foreign starkness (black "touched with silver," "a black and white check"). Finally, the "carnival costume complete with mask" seems most out of place, more in keeping with an island Mardi Gras or the "Masquerade" with "all colours of the rainbow," which Anna in *Voyage in the Dark* remembers from her West Indian childhood (184–7).[10]

Like Anna, who can only watch the "Masquerade" and not participate because she is not black, Miss Bruce can look at these dresses but not wear them because she is outside the world to which they belong. Though she is described as "quite an old inhabitant of the Quarter," she remains firmly English, outfitting herself and her apartment with solid clothing and furniture of an English kind. Her speech patterns are still distinctly English, for example, in the syntax of "Why should I not collect frocks?" and in the polite superiority conveyed in the word "such" in "I should never make such a fool of myself as to wear them" (5). She certainly does not appear to be speaking French in these passages. Though they are brief, elsewhere in her stories Rhys has characters move freely between English and French. But Miss Bruce's lack of connection with Parisians is not in itself remarkable. As Rhys herself pointed out years later:

> The "Paris" all these people write about, Henry Miller, even Hemingway etc. was not "Paris" at all—it was "America in Paris" or "England in Paris." The real Paris had nothing to do with that lot. . . . As soon as the tourists came the *real* Montparnos packed up and left. (*Letters*, 280)

Though Miss Bruce's outsider status in the French community is evident from the narrative, her insider status in the foreign community is less clear:

> She knew most people and was intimate with nobody. We had been dining and lunching together, now and then, for two years, yet I only knew the outside of Miss Bruce—the cool sensible, tidy English outside. (2)

At the story's end, the narrator says "we dined together at our restaurant," but there is no newfound intimacy following the discovery of Miss Bruce's wardrobe of dresses. The words "together" and "our" point to the habit not intimacy of their meetings. As in the circular patterning that Rhys uses in such stories as "La Grosse Fifi," "Till September Petronella," and, to the best effect, in *Voyage in the Dark* ["Ready to start all over again in no time," the doctor says after Anna's abortion (159)], Miss Bruce and the narrator are back where they started with the fulfillment of their broken three o'clock appointment. In a public place, they appear to talk about private matters. But Miss Bruce merely reinforces the preexisting image of herself. Offhandedly introducing the subject ["I suppose you noticed my collection of frocks?" (5)], she uses it to differentiate herself from the type of woman who would wear such dresses. Saying that she would not, she implies that those who would are fools. She gives her companion no chance to respond and turns her attention to another table. The story ends with " 'Not bad hands and arms, that girl,' said Miss Bruce in her gentlemanly manner" (5). This could simply be Miss Bruce's "artist's eye" at work, the same eye that is mentioned at the start of the story (1). But it can also be seen as a ploy to turn attention away from herself to someone else, from personal disclosure to the practice of her profession. She turns from intimacy and remains an outsider.

Yet the words "gentlemanly manner" focus attention back on Miss Bruce and remind one of an earlier reference to her "thoroughly gentlemanly intonation" (1). These "gentlemanly" qualities, coupled with her "large bones and hands and feet" (1) distinguish Miss Bruce from "the petites femmes" she encounters, and emphasize again her alienation from those around her.

> As for the others, the petites femmes, anxiously consulting the mirrors of their bags, anxiously and searchingly looking round with

darkened eyelids: "Those unfortunate people!" would say Miss Bruce. Not in a hard way, but broadmindedly, breezily: indeed with a thoroughly gentlemanly intonation. . . . Those unfortunate little people! (1)

But these "petites femmes," like Miss Bruce, are outsiders. They remind one of the protagonists of Rhys's novels. Marya, Julia, Anna, Sasha, and, to a certain extent, Antoinette, are all, despite their differences, "petites femmes" in their vulnerability and in their constantly seeming ill-at-ease. In "Illusion," the "petites femmes" are described as "anxiously consulting the mirrors of their bags, anxiously and searchingly looking round with darkened eyelids" (1). *What* they do does not set them apart from others so much as *how* they do it. There is nothing extraordinary in a woman checking her makeup in a mirror or looking around the restaurant where she sits. These gestures are so small, so commonplace among women that the only way the "petites femmes" are distinguished from anyone else is that they do them "anxiously."

Critics have frequently praised Rhys's economical use of words, and attention to seemingly insignificant repetitions of word or phrase reveals motifs that point to her preoccupation with several major concerns, all of which stem from the plight of the outsider. Often her outsider is marked by an inability to execute a simple task that seems to give others no problems. In "Illusion," Miss Bruce can buy attractive dresses, but not wear them. In "Tea with an Artist," Verhausen, who is described as being "mad as a hatter," can paint brilliantly, but cannot bear to sell his works. In "Learning to Be a Mother," a woman can give birth, but has to learn how to give affection to her child. Petronella ("Till September Petronella") is a chorus girl who can rehearse her one spoken line, but she is speechless on opening night. Miss Verney ("Sleep It Off Lady") falls, but quite simply cannot get up. Miss Bruce, the first in a long line of Rhys outsiders, is unable to do the simplest things. She is at once one of the "petites femmes" and yet cut off from them by class, nationality, and culture.

Miss Bruce's "gentlemanly" attributes suggest a deeper alienation— from her own sexual longings. "Going on all the time all round her were the cult of beauty and the worship of physical love: she just looked at her surroundings in her healthy, sensible way, and then dismissed them from her thoughts" (1). This is a story with no men in it, only women. In its world, Miss Bruce assumes almost masculine qualities: "her large bones and hands and feet" (1); her slightly mannish clothes (2); her surname, which is a man's first name; her twice-noticed "gentlemanly" qualities; the way in which she inspects both "pretty women" and the "petites femmes." The solid, dark wardrobe in which she secretly collects symbols of feminine beauty may stand for a private self which she must conceal both from herself and others. The homoerotic element in Miss Bruce's character and fascinations is integral to the story and adds another layer of estrangement from self and desires to the protagonist and the story.

Miss Bruce is both the outsider and insider, public figure and private, "gentlemanly" woman and one of the "petites femmes." For all that she is thoroughly English, her hidden dresses introduce an exotic element, a flirtation with another world and life which she can purchase but never fully own. She cannot cross over into this world (complete with makeup and perfumes) any more than she can integrate even one article of it into her Englishness. She cannot, as it were, "go native" as Ramage, who seems to in "Pioneers, Oh, Pioneers" and as a consequence is lost to both white and black society in the West Indies (279). At the same time, Miss Bruce's temptation to do so, to abandon her Englishness, however unfulfilled that may be, sets her apart from thoroughly English types, such as the Eliots in "Pioneers, Oh, Pioneers," who rename their estate on the "Imperial Road" Twickenham (278) and to whom the thought of "going native" would never occur.

Short as it is, "Illusion" can be divided into three parts. The first two are of roughly equal length and make up all but the concluding paragraphs of the story. The first part consists of a description of Miss Bruce's Englishness. She is likened to "some sturdy rock" (1) and her wardrobe, as an extension of her character, is a suitably "solid piece" for her "solid coats and skirts" (3). This description of Miss Bruce's Englishness ends with the narrator's summation that she valued "solidity and worth more than grace or fantasies" (3). The key is then turned and our vision of Miss Bruce changes drastically. The second part of the story begins with a description of Miss Bruce's very un-English collection of dresses and of the fantasies and flirtation with otherness and other worlds which they suggest. Suddenly, the Miss Bruce of "solidity" is seen as a Miss Bruce "with the perpetual hunger to be beautiful and that thirst to be loved which is the real curse of Eve" (3–4) (words that could serve as the defining characteristics of the "petites femmes" she so looks down on). The third part, the final paragraphs of the story, does not reconcile the two previous ones. The conflicting images of Miss Bruce remain. Her few words aimed at reinforcing the initial image of her "solidity" and Englishness serve rather to draw attention back to the hidden dresses. "I should never make such a fool of myself as to wear them," she says (5), as if a dress makes a fool and all one has to do is wear the dress of the "petites femmes" to become one. Miss Bruce remains an outsider to the last, alienated from Englishness, from the otherness she longs for, from the "petites femmes," who are beneath the surface so like her, from the narrator who knows her story, from her own desires. And the narrator too is an outsider. She has penetrated Miss Bruce's inner sanctum, but achieves no intimacy. Her own surmises about Miss Bruce's feelings when buying the dresses suggest that she too shares her subject's alienated, divided self.

> Wonderful moment! When the new dress would arrive and would emerge smiling and graceful from its tissue paper.
> "Wear me, give me life," it would seem to say to her, "and I will do my damnedest for you!" And first, not unskillfully, for was she not a portrait painter? Miss Bruce would put on the powder, the Rouge Fascination, the rouge for her lips, lastly the dress—and she would gaze into the glass at a transformed self. She would sleep that night with a warm glow at her heart. No impossible thing, beauty and all beauty brings. There close at hand, to be clutched if one dared. Somehow she never dared, next morning. (4)

How does the narrator know if she has not gone through the same experiences herself in some form? The narrator is the final figure in Rhys's first and already comprehensive picture of outsiders.

"Mannequin"—Belonging

Of all Rhys's short stories, "Mannequin" stands out as much for what is uncharacteristic as for what is characteristic of her writing. It begins with the brevity that is Rhys's hallmark: "Twelve o'clock. *Déjeuner chez* Jeanne Veron, Place Vendome" (20). Although the story that follows is told in the third person, the similarity between this opening and a diary entry helps create a sense of intimacy and also helps to feed the Carole Angier school of critics, for whom all Rhys's writing is rehashed autobiography.[11] But what we also see in this passage is an easy flow from the use of one language to another which recurs throughout Rhys's writing and which is used perhaps to its best advantage in the scenes with Roseau and Fifi in "La Grosse Fifi." It also emphasizes a particular time and place. What follows is a description of the protagonist.

> Anna, dressed in the black cotton, chemise-like garment of the mannequin off duty was trying to find her way along dark passages and down complicated flights of stairs to the underground from where lunch was served.
>
> She was shivering, for she had forgotten her coat, and the garment that she wore was very short, sleeveless, displaying her rose-coloured stockings to the knee. Her hair was flamingly and honestly red; her eyes, which were very gentle in expression, brown and heavily shadowed with kohl, her face small and pale under its professional rouge. She was fragile, like a delicate child, her arms pathetically thin. It was to her legs that she owed this dazzling, this incredible opportunity. (20)

Anna in "Mannequin" is not only a recognizable prototype for Anna Morgan in *Voyage in the Dark*, but for a line of Annas and other "petites femmes." She wears black, a virtual trademark of the Rhys heroine. Anna Morgan in *Voyage in the Dark* and Marya Zelli in *Quartet* are both distinguished as "petites femmes" by their black dresses. Even the elderly and alcoholic writer in "The Lotus" reveals her connection with Rhys's younger heroines in her black dress whose front is "grey with powder" (211). When she runs naked through the street, it is as if, like so many other of the heroines, she imagines she can escape her misery by changing or shedding her black dress. In fact, she merely changes one imprisonment for another, ending with a policeman's black cape wrapped round her. Black as the uniform of the vulnerable, probably doomed "petite femme" recurs in "Tigers Are Better-Looking." Maidie Richards recalls a girl she spends the night with in jail.

> . . . a very dark girl. Rather like Dolores del Rio, only younger. But it isn't the pretty ones who get on—oh no, on the contrary. For instance, this girl. She couldn't have been prettier—lovely she was. And she was dressed awfully nicely in a black coat and skirt and a lovely clean white blouse and a little white hat and lovely stockings and shoes. But she was frightened. She was so frightened that she was shaking all over. You saw somehow that she wasn't going to last it out. (186)

Not only does the girl's dress remind us of Anna in "Mannequin," but her frailty is part of the earlier character's appearance too, and indeed of the whole line of Rhys's heroines. As opposed to Miss Bruce in "Illusion," Anna the mannequin is "fragile, like a delicate child, her arms pathetically thin" (20). She will "wear the *jeune fille* dresses" (20) she is told to because she can play no other role. But also like the girl in jail, Anna's future and her outlook on it is grim. After her first day as a mannequin, she says to herself that she "won't be able to stick it" (25).

Indeed, she has few illusions. Her vulnerability is as apparent to herself and to others as Lotus Heath's nakedness ("The Lotus"). When in the later story, Lotus's neighbor looks out the window and says, "But she's got nothing on," he is stating the obvious (218). Lotus cannot conceal herself any more than she can escape her condition. But "Mannequin" is less about escape than belonging, and this makes it stand out in Rhys's fiction. Anna finds a place, finds companions, and finds a role. At the end of the story, however temporarily, she belongs and has stopped being an outsider.

The story concerns a young girl's first day on the job as a model (a mannequin) for a French fashion house. It begins with the girl going to lunch, a rather banal point of entry, but one that affords opportunities for Rhys to show the uncommon difficulty of ordinary things for the "petite femme" heroine who is invariably an outsider. Anna is seen "trying to find her way along dark passages and down complicated flights of stairs to the underground from where lunch was served" (20). She "despaired of ever finding her way" as she encounters "countless puzzling corridors and staircases, a rabbit warren and a labyrinth" (21). Almost like Alice in *Alice in Wonderland*, her experiences are "dream-like" (21). She seems to have entered a world different from the one she is accustomed to, one in which appearances and realities, public facade and what lies behind it, conflict glaringly. The front of the salon is "wonderfully decorated," whereas the back has "an unexpected sombreness" (21). Like Alice in her fall down the rabbit hole and through various passageways, after which she finds herself at the Mad Hatter's table, Anna goes beyond the looking-glass perfect world at the front of the salons in her descent to the mannequins' lunch table.

> She pushed a door open.
> She was in a big, very low-ceilinged room, all the floor space occupied by long wooden tables with no cloths. . . . She was sitting at the mannequin's table, gazing at a thick and hideous white china

plate, a twisted tin fork, a wooden-handled stained knife, a tumbler
so thick it seemed unbreakable. (22).

Like a Mad Hatter at the head of the table sits "Madame Pecard,
the dresser," who is seen "talking loudly, unlistened to" (23). The
contradictory nature of the mannequins' world, of this place based on
the illusions of beauty, is evident in the juxtaposition of "loudly" and
"unlistened." Furthermore, when Madame Pecard insists that "It was
against the rules of the house for the mannequins to smoke. . . . The
girls all lit their cigarettes and smoked" (24–5). The contradictions
continue when the narrator informs us in contiguous sentences that
"Elaine was the star of the collection" and "Elaine was frankly ugly"
(23). Paradoxically, it is behind the scenes in this fashion house, which
uses women as types, for their physical attributes ("mannequin" suggests something not quite human, a dummy for hanging clothes on),
that Anna experiences something like companionship, acceptance, belonging among other women. "As they went out Babette put her arm
round Anna's waist and whispered: 'Don't answer Madame Pecard.
We don't like her. We never talk to her. She spies on us. She is a
camel' " (25). The outsider is a member of the club at last. During
lunch the mannequins talk about men, English men though they are
themselves French, about London though they are in Paris, and about
their ambitions to leave for jobs in London, in contrast to Anna, whose
hope it is to work at Jeanne Veron's in Paris. "A forlorn hope," she
says. But it turns out to be one that is fulfilled.

Herein lies a major difference between "Mannequin" and so many
of Rhys's other stories. "Mannequin" begins with a wish and ends with
its fulfillment. Anna wants the job and gets it. For all her exhaustion at
the end of the day, she is satisfied, "her fatigue forgotten, the feeling
that now she really belonged to the great, maddening city possessed
her and she was happy" (25–6). A protagonist's attaining happiness,
or even the use of the word "happy" with reference to one, is so
rare in Rhys's writing that it is worth noting when and under what
circumstances it occurs.

In three instances in Rhys's fiction, happiness is connected with
motherhood. In "Learning to Be a Mother," it takes some time for
the protagonist to "learn" how to love her child. When she does,
however, her feelings are unmistakable. "I was happy" (58). So too,
in *Good Morning, Midnight*, Sasha recalls her pregnancy in terms of
happiness.[12] In "Vienne," Francine says, "I was cracky with joy of life

that summer of 1921" (121), a summer in which she has money, a husband, and a baby on the way. Even in "The Day They Burned the Books," something like domesticity is a source of happiness. After saving a book from the fire, the child protagonist conceals it beneath her dress where, like a child in the womb, it "felt warm and alive" (155). "I felt very happy," she says. Happiness comes with permission to enter a London acting school in "Overture and Beginners Please." "I was happier than I'd ever been in my life," she declares. "Nothing could touch me, not praise, nor blame. Nor incredulous smiles" (320). In each of the above cases, happiness comes from a sense of belonging. Whether to a company of actors, mannequins, mothers, or wives, belonging and happiness are intertwined. Through belonging to some part of society, one's connection with and place in the world is secured. One is no longer a perpetual outsider. Once Anna becomes a mannequin, she has a place within the world of Paris as well. Her happiness is not just because she has a job; "the feeling that now she really belonged to the great, maddening city possessed her and she was happy" (25–6). The nature of this happiness is alluded to in the name of the street along which Anna walks, "the rue de la Paix" (25). It is the quiet happiness of a peace that comes from being accepted. Anna is driven by a desire to belong, to be accepted, and has her wishes fulfilled however briefly. Her "passionately grateful glance" to a customer who gives her approval may seem excessive, but for Anna such approval is a vital counterbalance to the cruelties of the day. "For, if the *vendeuse* Jeannine had been uniformly kind and encouraging, the other, Madame Tienne, had been uniformly disapproving and had once even pinched her arm hard" (25). Throughout the story, Rhys economically conjures a state of mind teetering on the edges of happiness and desolation. Jeannine intuitively understands this when she finds Anna emotionally and physically exhausted at the end of her first day and whispers to her, "Madame Veron likes you very much. I heard her say so" (25). The balance swings toward kindness again; Anna forgets her fatigue and is happy.

But there are few Jeannines waiting in the wings in Rhys's writing and few moments of belonging like those Anna enjoys with her or the other mannequins. Cruelty and exclusivity are the defining features of this world, as in the contempt that the well-off speaker in "Discourse of a Lady Standing a Dinner to a Down-and-Out Friend" feels for her (silent) interlocutor. Feelings of exclusion and rejection are the stuff of experience for Rhys's outsider heroines like Petronella or Inez or Selina. Except perhaps for Selina in Holloway, there are no moments of acceptance of belonging. Anna craves these and, unusually for Rhys's fiction, is granted them briefly.

But one should not idealize the salon in "Mannequin." It has its dangers, which Anna is, in this like so many Rhys heroines, seemingly ill-equipped to defend herself against. She starts out as the representative Jean Rhys outsider, lost in the maze of passageways behind the salon's fancy exterior. In her (typical) black chemise, she is "too shy to ask her way" (22), not knowing whom to trust and not wishing to appear more vulnerable than she does already. Initially, she is ignored by the other mannequins. "Coldly critical glances were bestowed upon Anna's reflection in the glass. None of them looked at her directly . . ." (21). Later she is "hustled into a leather coat and paraded under the cold eyes of an American buyer" (21). If she meets with approval from the sympathetic Jeannine, she encounters only coldness, disapproval, and pinching fingers from the other sales staff (22, 25). The "raking eyes of the customers" make her want to escape. " 'I will one day. I can't stick it,' she said to herself. 'I won't be able to stick it.' She had an absurd wish to gasp for air' " (25). Anna's burning desire for acceptance—"Was that all right?" (22)—receives a decidedly mixed response. To the American buyer who expresses approval of her, she gives "a passionately grateful glance" (25).

Yet shortly afterward, a few whispered words of encouragement from Jeannine make her intensely happy. Underlying these words is an acceptance of Anna as no different from any of the other mannequins. Anna's words of desperation express her feelings of isolation, her outsider status, in the repetition of the first-person singular pronoun: "I will [rush away] one day. I can't stick it. . . . I won't be able to stick it" (25). For what Jeannine's words lack in eloquence, they make up for in their inclusion of Anna with her use of "we." "We are all so. But we go on" (25). (Jeannine's motherly comforting of Anna makes her a predecessor of the older women who comfort and support heroines in "Learning to Be a Mother," "La Grosse Fifi," and "Outside the Machine.") The saleswoman's words echo the inclusive "we" in Babette's whispered sentences to Anna as she embraces her and welcomes her, as it were, into the sorority of mannequins: "We don't like her. We never talk to her. She spies on us" (25). Jeannine's and Babette's words indicate a solidarity, a belonging for Anna. However vague and fragile this is, Anna's belonging is a rare instance of a Rhys protagonist's being understood by and accepted into some group. But there are strong hints that Anna's happiness will be short-lived:

> All up the street the mannequins were coming out of the shops, pausing on the pavements a moment, making them as gay and as beautiful as beds of flowers before they walked swiftly away and the Paris night swallowed them up. (26)

The comparison of the mannequins to flowers lends the scene an impermanence even before we learn that "the Paris night swallowed them up." Anna's sense of belonging is as fragile and as transient as a bed of flowers in the city with its bustle and commerce and male power over women.

Anna's belonging also entails a separation from others. Like the hidden dresses in Miss Bruce's wardrobe, the mannequins, like "gay and beautiful" flowers stand out in and apart from their surroundings. But they also stand apart from the other women in the fashion house—"the sewing girls," "the workers," "the saleswomen" (23)—whose existence is based on labor and productivity rather than on the illusions of youth and beauty. Though the mannequins are inextricably linked to the other women, they are set apart because of the nature of their jobs. It may seem paradoxical that, in a story in which the protagonist attains a sense of belonging, she is merely joining the ranks of an isolated group. But for all that Anna is set apart from the others, she is, however temporarily, not alone. Above all, far from being despised, she is "envied" along with the other mannequins (23). In contrast to Inez in "Outside the Machine," who is a permanent outsider among the other English patients and who fears that they will say, "Useless, this one" because she does not fit in (193), Anna has a use and a function. Rhys is a writer intensely preoccupied with the trials of transient individuals who often have no fixed address or place of employment, but it is worth noting that the exceptions in her fiction often do belong by virtue of their usefulness or function in society, such as women in the role of wife ("Vienne") or mother ("Learning to Be a Mother"). As a mannequin, Anna has a function and place within the hierarchy of the fashion house, which she sees as giving her a place within French society as well ["the feeling that now she really belonged to the great, maddening city possessed her" (25–6)].

But Rhys never ignores the limits of these moments of happiness and belonging. In "Vienne," the husband goes broke; in "Learning to Be a Mother," belonging exists against a background of female pain and male power; in "Let Them Call It Jazz," solidarity and belonging exist only in jail, and the product of it, Selina's song, will be taken by a man and turned into a commercial product. Similarly, Anna's belonging involves complicity in an institution which, although run by a woman, sets women against women and fixes the mannequins in limited and particular roles (the "jeune fille," the "femme fatale," the "garconne"). And in the end, it is all as fragile as flowers on a city street. Paris will swallow them. They can only belong as long as their beauty lasts and they please the predominantly male buyers.

"La Grosse Fifi"—Brief Intimacy

On a first reading, "La Grosse Fifi" appears to be a typical story from *The Left Bank*. A narrator about whom we know nothing observes and tells us about one Fifi, about whom we know only slightly more. This is all done from the point of view of a female character, Roseau, about whom we have only a little more information. The setting is a hotel on the Riviera and, apart from three scenes in a particular hotel room, most of the story takes place in the public space of the hotel restaurant. "La Grosse Fifi" could thus be read as yet another story of outsiders, fleeting encounters, lack of intimacy, and the disparity between public face and private interior. Certainly, the scarcely known Fifi is, like Miss Bruce or Anna, a creator of illusions—that her gigolo is not paid to make love to her, and that his disappearance has to do with a sick grandmother.

> "Have you any news of Monsieur Rivière?" the *patronne* of the hotel would ask with a little cruel female smile.
> "Oh, yes, he is very well," Fifi would answer airily, knowing perfectly well that the *patronne* had already examined her letters carefully. "His grandmother, alas! is much worse, poor woman."
> For the gigolo had chosen the illness of his grandmother as a pretext for his abrupt departure.
> One day Fifi dispatched by post a huge wreath of flowers—it appeared that the gigolo's grandmother had departed this life.
> Then silence. No thanks for the flowers. (88)

The story's end also points to how little we know about Fifi. It is not until her death that we learn, from a newspaper report that Roseau reads, any more about her, such as her full name and age. Yet "La Grosse Fifi" is also about intimacy.

These hints of intimacy notwithstanding, the story starts and, for much of its length, continues as another study of outsiders. Both Roseau and Fifi are in similar ways set apart and set themselves apart from the various worlds through which they move. Roseau seems to belong nowhere. Indeed, the narrator is at pains over the first three pages to establish her outsider status. She is at least on the fringes of the Anglo-American community, although her name is a French word meaning "reed" (81). Her native language appears to be English, but she can read French well, as when she reads the article about Fifi's death, and she moves effortlessly between French and English in her conversations with Fifi. She is clearly not French, but her detachment when speaking about the English suggests she is no more English than she is American. The narrator distinguishes her from both. Roseau thinks of an "American acquaintance" or an "American lady's name" (82), implying that she is herself something else. She certainly annoys both Mr. Wheeler and Miss Ward by her behavior (82–3). Her distance from the English in the story is equally clear. Mark Olsen detects this from the start. He reflects, "this girl was a funny one, but he'd rather like to see a bit more of her" (79). The narrator repeats Olsen's "the funny one" two sentences later in the story. (Indeed, in Rhys's 1927 version of the text, it occurs a fourth time.) Despite his interest in Roseau, the Englishman is well aware of her oddness by his standards, and that his wife (with her very English name—Peggy) does not like her. Roseau stays in a "rum" hotel that he advises her against, "so full of odd-looking, very odd-looking French people with abnormally loud voices even for French people" (79–80). She knows about drinks he has never tried. " 'Have a Deloso,' said Roseau. 'It tastes of anis,' she explained, seeing that he looked blank" (80). She immediately sympathizes with Fifi while Olsen just as immediately finds her grotesque (80–1), and she deliberately sets out to shock him with her frankness about Fifi's gigolo. She further confounds Olsen's English prudery by insisting that gigolos also "exist in London." But, despite where she lives, she is not part of a French world either. She may attempt to bring Monsieur Leroy into a conversation, but later "The hotel seemed sordid that night to Roseau, full of gentlemen in caps and loudly laughing females. There were large lumps of garlic in the food, the wine was sour . . ." (83).

But it is above all from the English that the narrator and Roseau herself are concerned to distance themselves. From the moment Fifi appears, the Englishman's shock and hypocrisy are contrasted with Roseau's calm and acceptance. Olsen, whose own interest in Roseau is ambiguous (he wants "to see a little bit more of her" despite his wife's hostility), exclaims when he first sees Fifi:

> "Oh my Lord! What's that?"
> "That's Fifi," answered Roseau in a low voice and relaxing into a smile for the first time.
> "Fifi! Of course—it would be—Good Lord! Fifi!" His voice was awed. "She's—she's terrific, isn't she?"
> "She's a dear," said Roseau unexpectedly. (80)

Olsen's voice is shrill, marked by exclamations and broken syntax. But as his syntax breaks down, Roseau's builds to a point of clarity that is both patronizing and a parody of English calm. As if to define the word "gigolo" for him, Roseau explains, "She keeps him—he makes love to her" (81). Then, she adds, as a final crushing detail, "I know all about it because their room's next to mine" (81). This not only places Roseau in the company of the lovers (because she was overheard their lovemaking) but hints at some measure of defiant pride in this association.

Above all, Roseau means to shock. Her professed intimacy with Fifi's lovemaking is an invention. Later, when Fifi visits Roseau's room for the first time and explains that hers is next door, Roseau says, "Is it?" (83). She embellishes her knowledge of Fifi in order to shock the Englishman. Watching him squirm is empowering, but at a cost, for he leaves soon after. This is typical of both Roseau and her situation, and of other Rhys protagonists and their situations. Their isolation, their outsider status is in part brought about by rebellion, by a hitting out at their unjust, cruel, hypocritical environments. The consequences of such actions, however, are ostracism and marginalization.

Numerous Rhys heroines behave in this way and suffer similar consequences. Almost gleefully they expose people's hypocrisy and cruelty, and as a consequence they suffer ostracism, alienation, and loneliness. In "Let Them Call It Jazz," after Selina Davis throws a rock through a neighbor's window, provoked by pretensions about "white" respectability, she is sent to prison. In "Outside the Machine," after Inez

Best tells the other patients in the hospital ward "exactly what she thought about them, exactly what they were, exactly what she hoped would happen to them," they in turn reject her completely. Laura in "I Spy a Stranger" is hounded from her temporary home after she too has told enough people what she thinks of them and "got people against her" (244). Anna Morgan in *Voyage in the Dark* shows an early propensity for speaking her mind when she tells her very English stepmother, "I hate dogs" (71). Hester's response is to give her niece a lesson in hypocrisy. Think what you want, but say it and "People won't like you. People in England will dislike you very much if you say things like that" (71). Julia in *After Leaving Mr. Mackenzie* is someone who makes scenes because she is past caring what anyone thinks. Indeed, her only moments of calm are when she speaks her mind.[13] Just as Anna Morgan's stepmother does, so Julia's Uncle Griffiths wonders what will become of her as a consequence of such behavior (101). These Rhys protagonists are viewed by those about them as solely responsible for the unhappiness they suffer. Too obstinate to bend, too confrontational and tactless, they would do well to heed the words of the parson in "Outside the Machine," who warns the patients "against those vices which would antagonize their fellows and make things worse for them," such "vices" as self-pity, cynicism, and rebellion (196).

For such as Roseau, Selina, Inez, Anna, or Julia, rebellion is nearly always a verbal rather than a physical act. Even in "Let Them Call It Jazz," Selina's rock throwing is less liberating than the song she hears sung from the prison punishment cells which restores her to life (173). But what many critics view as the weakness, fecklessness, or general incompetence of Rhys's protagonists is often a form of rebellion.[14] There is certainly no lack of firmness and control in the words Roseau uses to shock Mark Olsen. They are no more the result of her naiveté with regard to social norms than they are the outcome of a passive, weak self overcome by a passing emotion. Contrasting with the Englishman's stammerings, Roseau's words are "coldly" delivered, clear, and complete. Her manner is equally composed in her argument with Mr. Wheeler (82). The Frenchman, M. Leroy, gives a defence of "strong emotion," but Roseau takes a more logical approach to winning the argument. Mr. Wheeler argues that nothing excuses the breaking of certain rules.

"But you excuse a sharp business deal?" persisted Roseau.
"Business," said Mr. Wheeler, as if speaking to a slightly idiotic
child, "is quite different, Miss . . . er . . ."
"You think that," argued Roseau, "because it's your form of emo-
tion."
Mr. Wheeler gave her up. (82–3)

Far from being "a slightly idiotic child," Roseau undermines Mr.
Wheeler's authority by a cold logic, knowing full well what she is
doing. And she suffers the consequences. M. Leroy can still be useful
("a good child") for fetching the gramophone, but Roseau is given up
and ignored, apart from the minatory "Lady Be Good" that her friends
play. The message is clear. If you defy or, worse, defeat authority and
respectability, you will be ostracized and rejected. Roseau's outsider
status, like that of other Rhys heroines, is won by defiance and rebellion, rather than passively acquired through feckless incompetence.

If Roseau is clearly one of Rhys's outsiders, Fifi is less obviously so.
She is clearly an object of fascinated derision to the English who encounter her, and she is one of the means whereby Roseau marks her
separation from them. Where the Olsens sneer, Roseau has immediate
sympathy with Fifi. But in her own French world, Fifi's status is less
clear. In many ways she is the presiding deity of Roseau's "rum" hotel.

> That long drab room looked ghostly in the flickering light—one had
> an oddly definite impression of something sinister and dangerous—
> all these heavy jowls and dark, close-set eyes, coarse hands, loud
> quarrelsome voices. Fifi looked sinister too with her vital hair and
> ruined throat. (89)

But she is far from secure in her belonging. In her appearance she is
an offense against conventional standards of female beauty, standards
which, we learn later, her gigolo shares.

> Fifi was not terrific except metaphorically, but she was stout, well
> corseted—her stomach carefully arranged to form part of her chest.
> Her hat was large and worn with a rakish sideways slant, her rouge
> shrieked, and the lids of her protruding eyes were painted bright
> blue. She wore very long silver earrings; nevertheless her face looked
> huge—vast, and her voice was hoarse though there was nothing but
> Vichy water in her glass. (80)

She seems to owe her position only to her ready money, and Roseau's denial of this to discomfit Peggy Olsen is hedged with ambiguity ("The man with the beard is host, I'm sure. He adores Fifi"). Once her gigolo leaves her, she must face "a hostile and sneering world" and the "little cruel female smile" of the *patronne*. Her ultimate defeat comes in the cruelly reductionist account of her murder, in which she becomes a set of numbers, an age, an address, and in which she is not allowed to speak for herself but only her murderer's self-justifying voice is heard. In the final analysis, she too is an outsider.[15]

In this public world of casual acquaintances and outsiders, there are hints of intimacy, although at times these are only of a false intimacy. Roseau spends her days with acquaintances whom she dislikes and with whom she has little in common. She exaggerates her closeness to Fifi and her knowledge of her lovemaking in order to shock Mark Olsen. The newspaper report pretends to bring its readers close to a murder, but gives only insignificant facts and only one account of events. Indeed, we as readers know little about the figures in the story. The very point of view that the narrator adopts is deceiving. So much is seen and experienced through Roseau, but finally so much is mysterious. What is the love affair that has reduced her to this state? Why do we learn so little about her past, her nationality, or even how she spends her time? The detective stories that Roseau asks Fifi to bring her usually involve the solving of murder mysteries. At the end of "La Grosse Fifi," we are left with a murder with only one partial explanation.

But there are moments of genuine intimacy in "La Grosse Fifi." The scenes in which Roseau and Fifi meet are pictures of human closeness and compassion rarely found in Rhys's writing. In the first, Roseau, after "three cachets of veronal," staggers around her hotel room late at night (83). It is immediately after her bitter encounter with Miss Ward and Mr. Wheeler. She feels "very tired, bruised, aching, yet dull as if she had been defeated in some fierce struggle." She seems to be trying to escape the hotel, either through drugged sleep or later by getting dressed and leaving. But Fifi comes to her door, "politely" asking about her health and advising her against going out (83–4). Fifi "spoke gently, coaxingly, and put her hand on Roseau's arm." What follows is altogether different from Roseau's verbal dueling with the English and Americans. Her guard is down. In response to Fifi's concern, she "collapsed on the bed in a passion of tears" (84). Fifi immediately assumes a motherly role toward Roseau. She helps her undress with ease and efficiency. As if Roseau were an extension of Fifi's own body, the latter is "not dismayed, contemptuous or curious" (84). She proceeds to offer hot milk (albeit with rum) and a kiss.

It seemed to Roseau the kindest, most understanding kiss she had ever had, and comforted she watched Fifi sit on the foot of the bed and wrap her flannel dressing-gown more closely round her. Mistily she imagined that she was a child again and that this was a large, protecting person who would sit there till she slept. (84)

The intimacy of the two women continues. Fifi reveals that she understands Roseau's sadness and its causes. She has seen and understood. "It's naturally a man who makes you unhappy" (84). " 'Yes,' said Roseau. To Fifi she could tell everything—Fifi was as kind as a God" (85). But Fifi too can make a confession. She speaks to Roseau with remarkable frankness—of her love for the gigolo, of her own ugliness. " 'I am old, I am ugly. Oh, I know. *Regarde moi ces yeux là!*' She pointed to the caverns under her eyes—*'Et ca!'* She touched her enormous chest. 'Pierrot who only loves slim women. *Que voulez-vous?* " (85). Language threatens to divide them when Roseau lapses into English, for Fifi "disliked foreign languages being talked in her presence" (85). But the next morning, in their second encounter, linguistic separation is overcome as the poem Fifi gives Roseau to read mixes English and French (86–7). Roseau's laugh after Fifi's departure may mark a closeness too (88). She laughs "long and very loudly for Roseau," recalling for the reader Fifi's own loud voice and laughter in the hotel restaurant.

Roseau's final intimate encounter with Fifi occurs the next morning. Already the intimacy is fading however. Roseau is already planning her departure from the hotel. She reflects, however, on how much she will miss her friend. "It was ridiculous, absurd, but there it was. Just the sound of that hoarse voice always comforted her; gave her the sensation of being protected, strengthened" (90). But at the same time, she is aware of how socially unacceptable Fifi is in Roseau's world, and how damaging their intimacy might be to her socially. At that moment Fifi arrives ready to go to meet the gigolo. Their last private conversation is frank. Roseau advises Fifi on her clothes, but advises her to pull her veil down. Outside the room there is no intimacy, but rather a separating veil. Roseau does not cry for Fifi when she reads the public newspaper report, but only when she turns to Fifi's book of poetry, token of their brief intimacy.

Intimacy is fleeting and limited, however, and Rhys refuses to let Roseau wallow in it [just as Roseau herself imagines Fifi's ghost "mocking her gently for her sentimental tears" (93)]. Roseau can only bear so much of Fifi's favorite verse. Earlier, a moment of supreme closeness, when Roseau feels most protected by Fifi's maternal shape, is interrupted by the violent creak of her bed under Fifi's weight and her ensuing curse (84). Later, the limits of Fifi's advice to Roseau and of how much help she can give her become apparent. Concerning the man who is the source of Roseau's happiness, Fifi says, ". . . do it first. Put him at the door with a *coup de pied quelque part*" (85). Roseau's response that she does not have a door shows both the inadequacy of Fifi's advice and also the source of Roseau's vulnerability and outsider status. "But I haven't got a door. . . . No vestige of a door I haven't— no door, no house, no friends, no money, no nothing." Fifi cannot supply her with a door or money, the lack of which has brought Roseau to her present circumstances. In the world of Rhys's fiction, it is usually only men who have doors, houses, friends, and money, and all that means. Even Fifi, who has money, leaves her new friend for the gigolo, and herself becomes a victim of male power, even her loud voice reduced to silence in the cold prose of the newspaper report.

For all its cruelty and coldness, the world of Rhys's fiction does show figures who parallel however briefly the intimacy of Fifi and Roseau, although always, as in "La Grosse Fifi," the limits of such intimacy are stressed. For example, Madame Tavernier's relationship with Inez Best is also that of a mother figure whose words of comfort express her compassion but provide no tangible solutions except in the short term. Even Inez's gratitude for Madame Tavernier's money is short-lived. The story ends with the bitter reflection that "you can't die and come to life again for a few hundred francs. It takes more than that. It takes more, perhaps, than anybody is ever willing to give" (209). Madame Laboriau in "Learning to Be a Mother" also recalls Fifi. Just as Fifi exhibits calm efficiency in helping Roseau to bed, the midwife is "so calm, so efficient" (57). Like Fifi, she is described as "fat" and has a liking for "brightly coloured dresses of velvet" under her overalls. Her compassionate composure stands in contrast to that of the mannish nurse, Miss Wyatt, in *After Leaving Mr. Mackenzie* who lacks any compassion (69). Although there are considerable limits to how much Madame Laboriau can ease the pain of the women under her care, she is verbally comforting to the narrator, who is frightened by her lack of instinctual motherly love. "That will come, that will come," she says (58). Observing the suffering round about them, the midwife says, "Like you: like me . . .," thus creating a bond between the narrator and herself and the other women. "Suddenly I realized that I was happy," the narrator says some time later. Although the link between Madame Laboriau's comforting words and the narrator's feelings of affection for her baby are not explicitly drawn in the text, the midwife does provide her with a sense of inspiration ["I had grown to admire her" (57)] and belonging.

While these figures lack the same degree of intimacy of the younger women, they do recall Fifi. She may be less of an inspiration to Roseau than a frightening prefiguring of what the protagonist may become, but she too, in those brief moments of intimacy in Roseau's room, fills the role of a motherlike provider of advice, comfort, and happiness. Roseau feels that "It was impossible not to be glad in that large and beaming presence" (90). It comes as no surprise that after Fifi's death, Roseau's first thought is "I must leave this hotel" (92). The bond between them broken, there is no reason for her to stay.

In England

"Till September Petronella"—Class Struggle

Petronella Gray is staying at a country cottage with Marston, an upper-middle-class painter, his music critic friend, and another woman who, like herself, lacks any background resembling the men's. Early on in the visit, Marston spells out her position, or lack of one, by asking her, "What's going to become of you, Miss Petronella Gray, living in a bed-sitting room in Torrington Square, with no money, no background, and no nous? . . . Is Petronella your real name?" (130). When she says yes, he does not believe her (it is presumably far too aristocratic a name for the likes of her), and indeed does not believe that she has any family at all. "Oh, you've got a grandmother, have you?" he sneers (130–1). Because she does not belong to his world, he has no interest in imagining any other world. For Marston, Petronella is a temporary diversion; lacking any real future with him (a permanent relationship is inconceivable), she can have no past either. But it is exactly that, her past, her social background, which determines everything between them. "Till September Petronella" is a report from the class war. Its characters may be rootless and vulnerable women of the London demimonde and their upper-middle-class sponsors, but it lays bare the forces of wealth and social class in women's experience in a much more general sense.[16]

In various exchanges between the other model, Frankie, and the gentleman music critic, Julian, the trappings of each one's different place in society are made clear repeatedly. These serve not only to illustrate the nature of their own relationship, but that of Petronella and Marston, and of a whole nation divided along class lines. "You're always going on about respectable people," Frankie tells Julian, "but you know *you* are respectable, whatever you say and whatever you do, and you'll be respectable till you die, however you die, and that way you miss something, believe it or not" (136). Just as Julian cannot change himself or his background, neither can Frankie. She sees through the falsity of his plans to have her "educated" by his mother "in her dreary house in the dreary country" (137) before being allowed to return to London. She knows that this is not an earnest attempt to do a Pygmalion with her, but to get rid of her after she fails to meet their standards of respectability. Petronella may love Julian, but the gap between them can never be bridged. To him, she can never be anything but "fifth rate," a "ghastly cross between a barmaid and a chorus girl," a "female spider" who is only after Marston's money (136–7).

Neither Frankie nor Petronella belong with these three men, any more than they belong in the countryside they are visiting. They are utterly confined to their roles as tarts and sponsors. When Petronella leaves, literally, through a window, the suffocating nature of her relationship with the others is highlighted. Not respectable enough or tart enough, she finds herself fitting nowhere. Like the young model in "Mannequin," whose exhaustion after the scrutiny of customers and employers makes her want to "rush away . . . rush away anywhere . . . [and] gasp for air," Petronella hurries back to London to escape their jibes (25). In Rhys's earlier story "A Night," the nightmarish spectacle of a jibing humanity could easily apply to Petronella's country companions.

> Their eyes are mean and cruel, especially when they laugh.
> They are always laughing, too: always grinning. When they say something especially rotten they grin. Then, just for a second that funny little animal, the Real Person, looks out and slinks away again. . . . Furtive. (47)

The response to all this of the speaker in "A Night" similarly anticipates Petronella's. "I don't belong here. I don't belong here. I must get out—must get out," the earlier character intones (47). She too tries to escape a living suffocation; she talks of "sitting up in bed, gasping" (48).

Although Petronella leaves Marston's company to return early to London, she cannot escape the social forces that Marston and Julian represent. The easiest way to get to London is in the car of a gentleman farmer who will take her to the railway station. He too has the trappings of wealth and power—a car, the social standing to have a lady pub owner do his bidding, a large silver cigar case, and the money for a bottle of Cliquot, a box of chocolates, and the first-class train fare too. For him, as well as for Marston and Julian, there is only one role for

Petronella, that of entertainer and perhaps future mistress. "I'd like to feel that when I go up to Town there's a friend I could see and have a good time with. You know" (141). He will buy her with "pretty dresses and bottles of scent, and bracelets with blue stones in them" (141). For Petronella, there does not seem to be any other choice. When Petronella arrives in London, she at once meets a man whose taxi she shares and who bears a marked resemblance to Marston. This one's name is Melville, but like Petronella's previous two protectors, he too has the money and authority that go with a similar social position. The exchanges with the taxi driver reveal his social class. After Petronella decides that she would rather go to Hyde Park than straight back to her boarding house, Melville shouts, "Not Torrington Square." As a result the driver stops the taxi and confronts him.

> "Here, where am I going to? This is the third time you've changed your mind since you 'ailed me."
> "You'll go where you're damn well told."
> "Well where am I damn well told?"
> "Go to Marble Arch."
> "Yde park," the driver said, looking us up and down and grinning broadly. Then he got back into his seat.
> "I can't bear some of these chaps, can you?" the young man said.
> When the taxi stopped at the end of Park Lane we both got out without a word. The driver looked us up and down scornfully before he started away. (145–6)

Responding to the working-class driver's lack of deference, Melville's words reaffirm his position of superiority, first with the retort "You'll go where you're damn well told," and then with the impersonal imperative "Go to Marble Arch." When the driver translates the latter as "Yde Park," not only is he reaffirming his own class background, but his lack of deference, which is further shown by his facial expressions. In this little skirmish in the class war, Petronella occupies an uneasy middle ground. Her use of "Hyde Park," as opposed to both "Yde Park" and "Marble Arch," places her apart from both these representatives of polarized segments of society. However, although she may seem aligned with the upper-middle-class Melville by the driver's scorn, and by Melville's invitation to look down on the driver, she must also bear Melville's "amused and wary, but more wary than amused" response to her. His attitude of caution toward her is rather like that of a man guarding his wallet from a possible pickpocket. He relaxes from time to time, but then his caution reasserts itself. Later, when Petronella asks him to bring her a gold bracelet, he is described as "wary again" (149). Prior to this, his caution makes him literally speechless, at the same time that he tries to express his interest in Petronella. " 'We must see each other again. . . . Please. Couldn't you write to me at—.' He stopped. 'No I'll write to you. If you're ever— I'll write to you anyway' " (149).

The inequalities in any future relationship between these two is foreshadowed already in that he knows where to find her, but she has no way of knowing how to find him. One is reminded of the inequalities in Anna's relationship with Walter Jeffries in *Voyage in the Dark*. When asked what her lover does for a living, Anna's reply reveals her limited knowledge about him because "he doesn't talk much about himself" (39). This, coupled with his avoidance of Anna's apartment, causes Anna's more experienced friend Maudie twice to call him "the cautious sort." "It's not such a good sign when they're like that" she adds (39). In "Till September Petronella," Melville is similarly unwilling to be seen with Petronella on her own turf. Like Jeffries, he has no interest in slumming in that way. But neither is he prepared to take Petronella into his own society (nor, of course, were Marston or the gentleman farmer). The private club serves as a safe haven where they can meet, dine, and sleep together without the risks of a too public restaurant or too private apartment.

> And everything was exactly as I had expected. The knowing waiters, the touch of the ice-cold wine glass, the red plush chairs, the food you don't notice, the gold-framed mirror, the bed in the room beyond that always looks as if its ostentatious whiteness hides dinginess. (148)

The private club embodies the many restrictions and illusions of relationships like that of Anna and Jeffries or of Petronella and Melville. It provides the safety of anonymity, yet the waiters are described as "knowing." It affords them the privacy for intimacy, yet this intimacy is merely physical. Dinner is a formality, and the food goes unnoticed. The predictability of the lavish decor ("everything was exactly as I had expected") dulls any pleasure which it might have evoked, being only an indicator of the man's wealth, class position, and intentions for the evening. Like the bed, whose "ostentatious whiteness hides dinginess," the private club with its veneer of respectability and splendor, is merely a venue for the sordid business of buying sex. Above all it is a venue that belongs to Melville not to Petronella. She invites him to a place she knows, "The Apple Tree," where, she tells him, "You could come as my guest. I'm a member. I was one of the first members" (147). Melville plays with the idea, and then says, "Oh, damn the Apple Tree. I know a better place than that" (148). He cannot tolerate any diminution of his power and authority.

But it must be insisted that Petronella is by no means merely a spineless, feckless semiwhore. As Melville seems to take control, Petronella by contrast might seem wholly passive. But Rhys dispels this view of her from the start when she interrupts the exchanges between Melville and Petronella with Petronella's thoughts. "How do you know what's in what street? How do they know who's fifth-rate, who's fifth-rate and where the devouring spider lives?" (147). In fact, from the moment Petronella asks to change her destination in the taxi, she, not Melville, is seen to be stage-managing the events that follow. The theatrical parallels are most apparent in the final pages of the story. Relating an incident from her brief career as a chorus girl, Petronella draws a picture of herself as an inept actress unable to remember a single line. Afterward, she demands a gold bracelet from Melville and tells him not to "dare to come back without it" (149). The contrast in the two voices—when Petronella describes her old self, mute and insecure, and when she puts her demands to Melville—points to the part she is now playing, that of the mercenary tart. As if she has taken Marston's advice to sharpen her claws (131), there is a hardness about her even as she flirts with Melville. She speaks more like Frankie than herself. Unsuccessful as a stage aristocrat ["I rehearsed it and rehearsed it, but when it came to the night it was just a blank" (149)], she seems determined to get her part right this time.

Petronella's lack of emotional involvement in her dealings with Melville is conveyed by Rhys's use of reflections and flashbacks. The first create a sense of detachment. The second, in which Melville reminds her of Marston [*"But Marston should have said, 'It tastes of nothing, my dear, it tastes of nothing.' . . ."* (148)], generalizes her London encounter so that it is depersonalized. All three men she encounters are reduced to symbols of the powerful social class from which they come and to which Petronella is a permanent outsider. If Petronella is in a sense reduced by her encounters with these men, they too become interchangeable, social power and authority wearing slightly different masks.

But for all her exercise of power, for all her reduction of these men, Petronella is trapped at the end of the story. The action is circular— Petronella leaves London at the start and returns there at the end. From the very beginning, she wishes to escape and is depressed when her one friend, Estelle, does leave London for Paris. The pattern of Petronella's relations with men comes to mirror her feelings of exclusion as well as her entrapment within British society. The few things that she actually likes in Britain are *not* British. Rhys indicates this in the story's opening paragraph. "There was a barrel organ playing at the corner of Torrington Square. It played 'Destiny' and 'La Palome' and 'Le Reve Passe,' all tunes I liked, and the wind was warm and kind not spiteful, which doesn't often happen in London" (125). Petronella likes French music and warmer climates. She longs to be "like Estelle," who is French and whose room "didn't seem like a Bloomsbury bed-sitting room," but "like a room out of one of those long, romantic novels, six hundred and fifty pages of small print, translated from French or German or Hungarian or something" (125–6).

When Estelle leaves London, Petronella seems to lose her one possibility of escape. Images of her paradoxical entrapment within yet lack of connection with British society are represented in the aimless, long walks she takes "always the same way," in a ritual of hatred for all that she sees. Finally, her only solace she says is "that I could kill myself any time I liked and so end it" (126). Her wish to be like Estelle can be interpreted as a wish for a place to belong or go back to (i.e., Paris), and also as a wish for control. Estelle, she says, "walked the tightrope so beautifully, not even knowing she was walking it" (125). This is surely a metaphor for Estelle's control over her own life, a control that Petronella lacks and in part aspires to. But, with her, one is reminded of the desperate women in "Hunger" and "A Night," in which motifs of falling convey the speakers' social and emotional position on the brink of disaster. In the former story, the speaker reflects on her poverty and hunger: "It is like being suspended over a precipice. You cling for dear life with people walking on your fingers. Women do not only walk: they stamp. . . . Once down you will never get up. *Did* anyone—did *any*body, I wonder, ever get up . . . once down?" (43). In "A Night," she speaks of falling "down, down, down, for ever and ever. Falling," and of her longing "for something to hold on to. Or somebody" (48). Estelle may walk the tightrope, and Frankie stamp on a few hands, but one wonders if there is anything in store for Petronella but a fall.

Yet it is hard to see what more Petronella can do to save herself. Lacking background, love, friendship, money, she is an utter outsider within English society. The "No Models" signs in front of apartments sum up her exclusion (125). Yet she is also trapped within that society, without exit, without any place to return to, and without any role except that of chorus girl or tart. Petronella starts off the story as a social outcast, lonely and alienated, but the ending is even more disturbing. As she plays the part of a tart, the parallels between her relationship with Melville and that with Marston (and perhaps that with the farmer) suggest no departure or freedom from her past disappointments. There is no "good time coming for the ladies" (as Petronella's landlord ironically suggests), only more of the same. Indeed, the great world of historical events has a further turn of the screw for everyone. Both Marston and Melville cheerily say they will see Petronella again "in September" (143, 150). But this is July 28, 1914. By September the men will be going off to war.

"Let Them Call It Jazz" and "Outside the Machine"—On the Margins of Empire

> *Why, it's not a bit like that. My Lord, what liars these people are!*
> *And nobody to stand up and tell them so. Yah, Judas!*
>
> ("Outside the Machine," 201)

"Let Them Call It Jazz" and "Outside the Machine" differ substantially from each other. Written at different times in Rhys's career, they differ considerably in setting, and have protagonists who differ in terms of race and cultural background. Yet they have intriguing points of similarity, and can be usefully compared to reveal evidence of the coherent and consistent focus that runs through Rhys's short fiction over many years, and also of the generality—as well as the particularity—of her vision of human personal and social alienation. Selina Davis and Inez Best, the black West Indian immigrant in 1950s Britain and the white English woman in 1920s Paris, for all their differences, experience the exclusion and cruelty of English society in very similar ways. Marginalized by race and class, respectively, they are ignored and illtreated by a social structure that exists for the benefit of others and not theirs.

One bright Sunday morning in July I have trouble with my Notting Hill landlord because he ask for a month's rent in advance. He tell me this after I live there since winter, settling up every week without fail. I have no job at the time, and if I give the money he want there's not much left. So I refuse. The man drunk already at that early hour, and he abuse me—all talk, he can't frighten me. But his wife is a bad one—now she walk in my room and say she must have cash. When I tell her no, she give my suitcase one kick and it burst open. My best dress fall out, then she laugh and give another kick. She say month in advance is usual, and if I can't pay find somewhere else. (158)

So begins "Let Them Call It Jazz." With the possible exception of *Wide Sargasso Sea* (which opens with "They say when trouble comes close ranks, and so the white people did. But we were not in their ranks"), nowhere else in Rhys's writing is the protagonist so immediately portrayed as an outsider. It can be argued that Selina Davis is the ultimate outsider among all of Rhys's protagonists. This outsider status is established in several ways: through dialect and the language of prejudice; through plot; and through the protagonist's own reflections.

"Let Them Call It Jazz" is Rhys's only extensive and exclusive use of dialect, and the effect of this on the story is profound. It identifies the protagonist/narrator as a black West Indian and thus a member of a racial and ethnic minority in London. Furthermore, as it is sustained, it serves as a constant reminder of the speaker's race and ethnicity and of how both set her apart from almost everyone else she meets.[17]

The issue of race and prejudice is central to any discussion of the issue of belonging in "Let Them Call It Jazz." It is interesting to note, however, that racist insults are never used toward Selina as, for example, "nigger" is used in "The Day They Burned the Books." In fact, no one names or refers to Selina's race. The nearest anyone comes to this is when her neighbor says, "At least the other tarts that crook installed here were *white* girls" (167). Even here the attack is by omission. Just as her English neighbors have no word for her, so too England has no place for Selina Davis. She is outside their vocabulary, outside their culture, and outside their society. But a language of racist insult certainly exists in England, as it does for the Englishman who insults his black West Indian wife in "The Day They Burned the Books." Rhys does not overlook this, but rather points to a more insidious aspect of the abuse to which Selina is subjected. The superior attitude of her white English neighbors makes it beneath their dignity to give her race a name.

Vulgar racial insult is ignored as base in the same way that Selina's existence is ignored. While it is permissible to gawk, actual interaction is avoided. Thus Selina is effectively reduced to something less than human. In a sense, she ceases to exist, so deep is her rejection by white England. After she first moves into a "respectable" area in London, her power of human speech is effectively taken away from her by a neighbor's power to ignore: "There's no wall here and I can see the woman next door looking at me over the hedge. At first I say good evening, but she turn away her head, so afterwards I don't speak" (161). Her ability to interact is denied by her neighbors' denial of her very existence. When Selina seeks the help of one of them and knocks at her door, she "can hear her [the neighbor] moving about and talking but she don't answer" (166). As a result, she never tries the woman's door again.

Indeed, silence becomes the language of racial hatred and prejudice in "Let Them Call It Jazz." It contributes directly to Selina's isolation and ultimate segregation from English society. In her successive encounters with the police, after she is robbed of her savings (163–4), accused of disturbing the peace (165), and charged with breaking a window (168–70), there are no witnesses for the defense, no one who speaks on her behalf. The silence of her white English neighbors damns her case in a legal system that requires corroboration from others. As a consequence, her own rights as a victim of robbery are denied, she is fined, and ultimately serves a prison sentence. No one speaks to her and no one speaks for her. As Selina says at the beginning of the text, "if nobody see and bear witness for me, how to prove anything?" (158).

Plot and action also establish and constantly confirm Selina's outsider status. She is not unlike many of Rhys's protagonists who live in rented rooms. But Selina is unluckier than most in that she is made homeless through no fault of her own. Whereas many others, at least to some extent, *choose* to walk the streets of London or Paris, Selina has no choice. She is both figuratively and literally on the outside of English society, and nowhere is this more apparent than when she must "walk about" until a coffee bar opens, her landlady having evicted her without any warning one bright Sunday morning.

The pattern of her experience with English landlords follows from a lifetime of abandonment and loss. Her white father abandons her in her infancy (164), and the act is repeated again and again, her birthright effectively denied in each encounter with the English. For example, when Mr. Sims, a landlord and possible pimp, gives her a place to stay, he kisses her "like you kiss a baby," promising to return. Like her white father, he is never heard from again directly. Selina is left, with no function or future, in the shell of a once fine house fallen into disrepair with a garden overgrown with weeds and inedible fruit (160–61).

Here the echoes of a colonial experience are unmistakable—the paternalism and the plundered Eden. When another white Englishman turns Selina's song into a successful and (for him) profitable jazz tune, the colonial and postcolonial experience is complete. The song, which she hears in Holloway Prison, which speaks for all those locked up by and excluded from English society, and which comes to represent virtually her only moment of intimacy and belonging, is turned into a commodity for someone else's profit. She remembers "when that girl sing, she sing to me and she sing for me. I was there because I was *meant* to be there. It was *meant* I should hear it—this I *know*" (175). Although "the Holloway song," unlike her other songs, is not handed down to her from her grandmother, its source—prison, because it was her only other place of belonging—links it with her West Indian identity. She must lose this along with everything else in order to fit into English society. The cost of her assimilation is repeatedly experienced in terms of loss, not gain. "The Holloway Song" is the last thread in Selina Davis's identity. As if this manifested itself physically as well as psychologically and Selina Davis were as naked as the old woman running into the night in "The Lotus," the story concludes appropriately with her buying a dress with the money she has been given for the song.

When they call it jazz, the song becomes theirs, not hers. Similarly, when the Rochester figure in *Wide Sargasso Sea* renames his West Indian wife Antoinette with the heavy, Northern European name Bertha, she starts to lose all sense of herself. "Names matter," she reflects, "like when he wouldn't call me Antoinette, and I saw Antoinette drifting out of the window with her scents, her pretty clothes and her looking-glass" (180). Names matter in the history of colonization, in which the renaming of places and people is part of the act of conquering and controlling them. But whereas "the Holloway Song" is turned into jazz, the protagonist's name remains unaltered and unspoken. She is neither "nigger" nor "Selina Davis," but a nonperson, without presence or existence. Whereas the song finds a "place," the protagonist remains firmly on the margins of English society.

Interspersed with Selina Davis's account of her exclusion from English society are her reflections on the condition of England and on the English in general. Whether she refers to people as "English" or simply "they" and "them," the effect is that of an outsider looking in at another culture. Selina also speaks specifically of her lack of belonging. "I don't belong nowhere really," she insists, "and I haven't money to buy my way to belonging" (175). These reflections and observations serve two major functions in the text: they contribute to the reader's sense of intimacy with the speaker (in a world that denies her any intimacy), and they also, by their nature, generalize her experiences. She is passing judgment on all the English, with their slowness ["English people take long time to decide—you three-quarter dead before they make up their mind about you" (158)], their sweetly dangerous, politely crushing voices ["but I'm very suspicious of these quiet voices now" (169)], and their hideously dressed women ["She wear sandals and thick stockings and I never see a foot so big or so bad" (168)]. "They like that here," she reflects, "and better not expect too much" (174).

Except for the use of dialect, Rhys uses similar methods to present Inez Best as an outsider in "Outside the Machine" (the title says it all), whose parallels with "Let Them Call It Jazz" are so great that any discussion of one story invites a consideration of the other. In both stories the protagonists are outsiders for reasons beyond and within their control. Selina Davis is an outsider in English society because she is black, foreign, and poor. Inez Best is an outsider within the microcosm of English society that she experiences as a patient in an English hospital in Paris. Not only is the hospital run "on strictly English lines" by the nurses, but all social behavior is run on these lines by the patients. They make Inez almost instantly an outsider. The reasons for this are never clearly stated. To an extent, it may have to do with lack of money (Inez has nowhere to go and no money to support herself at the story's end). The very lack of specific reasons for her being "outside the machine," however, may help to generalize her situation. This is how the English treat all outsiders.

But factors within their control also link Selina and Inez. Both by their behavior contribute to their outsider status. In their aversion to what they see as a hypocritical politeness in the respectable, middle-class English, they are neither hypocritical nor polite in many of their relations with others. Both Selina and Inez tell people exactly what they think of them, in thoroughly clear and offensive terms. Inez, for example, finally gives vent to her feelings of contempt for the smug, superficial, and self-satisfied Englishwomen of different social classes who surround her. Mrs. Murphy's attempted suicide is the catalyst for the complete breakdown in her relations with all but Madame Tavernier. Inez strikes back at the cruel behavior of the middle-class Mrs. Wilson and the working-class Pat as they criticize Mrs. Murphy.

> Stone and iron, their voices were. One was stone and one was iron. . . .
>
> Inez interrupted their duet in a tremulous voice. "Oh, she's neurasthenic, and they've sent her to a place like this to be cured? That was a swell idea. What a place for a cure for neurasthenia! Who thought that up? The perfectly good, kind husband, I suppose."
>
> Pat said, "For God's sake! You get on my nerves. Stop always trying to be different from everybody else."
>
> "Who's everybody else?"
>
> Nobody answered. (204)
>
> . . . .
>
> The voice and the laughter were so much alike that they might have belonged to the same person. *Greasy and cold, silly and raw, coarse and thin; everything unutterably horrible.*
>
> "Well here's bad luck to you," Inez burst out, "you pair of bitches. Behaving like that to a sad woman! What do you know about her? . . . You hold your head up and curse them back, Mrs. Murphy. It'll do you a lot of good." (205)

Not only does Inez's and Selina's behavior show up and contrast with the cruelty marked by English politeness, it also sets them completely apart from the others. Yet, as is typical of most of Rhys's stories, there are few momentous occurrences in "Let Them Call It Jazz" and "Outside the Machine." The actions or verbal outbursts of the two protagonists do not decide their fates, but rather seal them. Their moments of truth merely confirm their lack of belonging. When Selina calls her neighbor "a dam' fouti liar" (167), and Inez tells the other patients, "This and that to the lot of you" (206), any door to their acceptance is slammed shut. But the door was scarcely open anyway; their behavior merely confirms the expectations of those around them.

In the case of both stories, we encounter typical Rhys outsiders, alienated, despised, ostracized by "decent" society, whose moments of rebellion only confirm the respectable world's low opinion of them. But in both cases, the text's focus is not only on the protagonist as outsider, but also on the protagonist's/outsider's view of the world that rejects her. We see the insiders judging the outsider, for sure, but also the outsider passing judgment on the insiders.

In both stories, those who belong are part of a larger institutional structure, represented by the English legal system in "Let Them Call It Jazz" and by the medical establishment in "Outside the Machine." Selina Davis's abusive landlords and neighbors can be seen to be part of a legal system that works entirely to their benefit, supporting their ability to evict, lie, insult, and ostracize at will. The system serves their interests, not Selina's, and certainly not those of justice. In the end, it locks away those who annoy its beneficiaries too much. The medical institution in which Inez finds herself scarcely allows her any place within it. Her time is limited there, and once it is past, she will be put on the street. Most of the time it treats her almost indifferently ["They moved about surely and quickly. They did everything in an impersonal way. They were like parts of a machine, she thought" (193)], although it is also capable of disapproval [" 'Can't you do without all those things while you are here?' the matron asked, meaning the rouge, powder, lipstick and hand-mirror on the bed table" (189)]. It can also ignore her completely when it wishes, just as Selina can be made a nonperson by her neighbors. The egregious Mrs. Wilson has just declared Inez to be a social and moral outcast. The doctor and nurse do not even respond to Inez with disapproval.

> The doctor blinked, but the sister's long, narrow face was expressionless. The two were round the beds glancing at the temperature charts here, saying a few words there. Best, Inez. . . .
> The doctor asked, "Does this hurt you?"
> "No."
> "When I press here does it hurt you?"
> "No."
> They were very tall, thin and far away. They turned their heads a little and she could not hear what they said. And when she began, "I wanted to . . ." she saw that they could not hear her either, and stopped. (206)

In addition, the patients (like Selina's neighbors) who are easily placed in English society and who act accordingly, fit in much better than Inez in the hospital. It is their institution, their machine.

> The women in the beds bobbed up and down and in and out. They too were parts of a machine. They had a strength, a certainty, because all their lives they had belonged to the machine and worked smoothly, in and out, just as they were told. Even if the machine got out of control, even if it went mad, they would still work in and out, just as they were told, whirling smoothly, faster and faster, to destruction. (193)

Inez is truly outside this machine. Whereas the two "aggressively respectable" blondes can talk endlessly about the weather, Inez has no capacity for chatter (191). Like two separate languages, Inez's is distinctly personal while the other English patients speak a largely impersonal and superficial one. There is a paradox in the lack of privacy in the hospital and the lack of any emotional intimacy between patients. Like the cafés and hotels of Rhys's other stories, the hospital is a public place where people come and go and are known only briefly and superficially. "[T]here was the one who wore luxury pyjamas, the one who knitted, the other constant reader . . . the one who had a great many visitors, the ugly one . . ." (200–1). Lack of privacy in the ward only highlights the lack of intimacy. For all they appear to share in the hospital (waking, bathing, eating, sleeping, and so on), Inez and the other patients share nothing. Ultimately, they are strangers who spy on and size one another up, desperate to place each other in the greater machine of the English social order, and prepared to viciously ostracize those like Inez or Murphy whom they cannot place and of whom they disapprove. While the two "aggressively respectable" blondes chatter about the weather, they are in fact scrutinizing the new patient in much the same way that Selina Davis's neighbors scrutinize her.

> Under cover of this meaningless conversation the fair woman's stare at Inez was sharp, sly and inquisitive. "An English person? English, what sort of English? To which of the seven divisions, sixty-nine subdivisions, and thousand-and-three subsubdivisions do you belong? (*But only one sauce, damn you.*) My world is a stable,

decent world. If you withhold information, or if you confuse me by jumping from one category to another, I can be extremely disagreeable, and I am not without subtlety and inventive powers when I want to be disagreeable. Don't underrate me. I have set the machine in motion and crushed many like you. . . ."

Madame Tavernier shifted uneasily in her bed, as if she sensed this clash of personalities—stares meeting in mid-air, sparks flying. . . .

"Those two ladies just opposite are English," she whispered. (192)

Selina Davis's experiences in "Let Them Call It Jazz" are almost completely devoid of intimacy with another human being. Her landlord and landlady, Mr. Sims, the neighbors, the police, the prison guards, all are distant or abusive. Even her fellow outcasts in Holloway are scarcely welcoming, and we know too little to judge of her relationship with her fellow West Indian Clarice at the story's end. Only for the short-lived moment of the song, does she feel any sense of closeness or belonging ["But when that girl sing, she sing to me and she sing for me" (175)]. But by the end of the text even this has been taken from her.

However, Rhys does allow Inez one of the limited experiences of intimacy that occur occasionally in her fiction, just as she does Roseau in "La Grosse Fifi." It is with Madame Tavernier. The older woman plays a very important role in the story. Shifting "uneasily in her bed" she bears witness to what otherwise might be thought of as Inez's lonely and paranoid rantings. She underscores Inez's perceptions of those around her and shows a humanity and kindness which the others lack. One can best see how Madame Tavernier is set apart from the others in the ward by her response to Inez's tears (198). Unlike the nurse who irritably scolds, "Now don't be silly," Madame Tavernier says, "Don't cry, don't cry," in a tone that is wholly nonjudgmental. The repetition modifies her use of the imperative, giving it a soothing effect. In the womblike atmosphere of the ward—"dark except for the unshaded bulbs tinted red," it is like a birth canal, "a long grey river; the beds were ships in a mist" (195)—Madame Tavernier is a mother figure to Inez. Incidental details, by their proximity to womblike images, reinforce one's sense of Madame Tavernier as a surrogate mother and Inez Best as a child. For example, on the morning following Inez's tears, Inez is denied breakfast and told, "Only milk for you today" (195). At the story's end, when Inez is discharged, Madame Tavernier lends her money wrapped in a handkerchief which, like her skin, smells of vanilla (209). This contrasts with the smell of turpentine in the halls of the hospital (202), and through its associations with baking further links Madame Tavernier with an albeit traditional image of the mother. The hospital's association with turpentine and Madame Tavernier's with vanilla points to their basic differences. The hospital, which is a microcosm of English society, is functional and machinelike. Even though it is run by human agents, these are depicted as soulless cogs in a larger machine. Madame Tavernier, on the other hand, is compassionate. But her gift of money, for all its generosity, is of limited practical help. While the narrator's response may seem ungrateful, it accurately points out the wider limitations of Madame Tavernier as a substitute mother. "Because you can't die and come to life again for a few hundred francs," Inez notes wryly (209). Like Inez (and Selina Davis in "Let Them Call It Jazz"), Madame Tavernier can effect no change in the system because she too is an outsider. Although she is grouped with the other English women, her French name and her speech set her apart. She "spoke English hesitatingly—not with an accent, but as if her tongue were used to another language" (190). Like Inez (whose name also sets her apart from the Pats and Mrs. Wilsons), Madame Tavernier is English but not of the English. She may be compassionate, but she too is outside the machine and consequently powerless.

It is the awful certainty and confidence, the hard, efficient lack of humanity and compassion of all the English women, nurses, respectable matrons, and dancers alike, that so grates on Inez (and the reader). Unlike these others, who "had a strength, a certainty, because all their lives they had belonged to the machine and worked smoothly, in and out, just as they were told" (193), Inez and Madame Tavernier exhibit a frailty and unease. Besides Mrs. Murphy, who is scorned for her failed suicide attempts, they are the only ones who shed a tear or exhibit any fear. The others, even in the face of another patient's death, give off an air of immunity, so great is their English self-confidence, which manifests itself in an indifference to others. By contrast, Inez lacks the confidence to ask the nurse if she might extend her stay in the hospital. Mrs. Murphy, who fears even the most casual eye contact with anyone (200), is an extreme example of what Inez might become. The patients recognize their similarities. "We were wondering if it was Murphy, or . . .," says Pat excitedly to Inez, clearly implying that they thought it might have been Inez who had attempted suicide.

That Mrs. Murphy is a mother, "with two sweet little kiddies" (203), makes her all the more reprehensible to the other patients. She is regarded as going against nature. But, as always in Rhys's fiction, the most ordinary things can be extraordinarily difficult for her "petites femmes," her outsider heroines. For Mrs. Murphy, the mother and life-giver, living is hard. For the old woman, Madame Tavernier, growing old is hard—she dyes her hair, she clings like a schoolgirl to a romantic letter from her husband, she trembles at the thought of death. For the Englishwoman, Inez Best, English words and conversations come hard, and English companions bring distress rather than the comfort of familiarity.

In both "Outside the Machine" and "Let Them Call It Jazz," the English of all classes exercise power over those outsiders they encounter. They judge and ostracize those who annoy them enough. The experiences and attitudes of Inez or Selina are literally beyond the imaginations of most of those they meet, even if they wanted to make the effort. The legal system is deaf to Selina's story; Inez's life is beyond the hospital's knowledge or interest. When the nurse discharging her tells Inez that "you must go straight to bed as soon as you get back," Inez thinks, "Get back where? . . . Why should you always take it for granted that everybody has somewhere to get back to?" (207). But these institutions also exercise power over the two protagonists. When Selina Davis is discharged from prison, she too has nowhere to go. In both "Outside the Machine" and "Let Them Call It Jazz," it is up to others, hospital or prison officials, how long you stay and when you leave, emphasizing the powerlessness of the protagonists and the power of those within the system. Their ability to decide on matters of life or death—they thwart Mrs. Murphy's and Selina's suicide attempts (171), as they would thwart any by Inez—lends them a godlike quality. But their inhumanity suggests that the world of the English is less a heaven, and more a hell-on-earth.

Not only does the machine, the system, and those who belong to it judge Inez and Selina, but Inez and Selina pass judgment on *them*. In "Outside the Machine," English inhumanity is depicted in terms of a mechanized hell. Individuals are reduced to "parts of a machine" (193). In "Let Them Call It Jazz," life in London is more akin to a Biblical hell, in which the traditional image of the heathen savage is stood on its head and it is the English who are "dam' devils" (171). In both systems, there is no attempt made to integrate the outsider. Belonging seems a matter of birth, not choice. Those who belong have done so "all their lives" (193), just as the white Londoner assumes superiority to the black West Indian immigrant as a birthright. Exclusion not inclusion is the rule. "Because she was outside the machine," Inez fears, "they might come along at any time with a pair of huge iron tongs and pick her up and put her on the rubbish heap, and there she would lie and rot" (193). Selina is asked by her neighbor, "*Must* you stay? *Can't* you go?" (164).

The neighbor's voice, like that of the policeman and magistrate, is very "quiet." But after a while, Selina becomes "very suspicious of those quiet voices," their softness like the hiss of a Biblical snake (169). In contrast Selina is repeatedly associated with noise (singing, shouting), and the text makes a correlation between loudness and truth and rebellion. Inez Best too speaks out loudly against her English companions. Similarly, the texts link quiet with hypocrisy, collusion, the status quo, and English society in general. Any attempt to speak for oneself or for others, to bear witness to humanity and against the quiet cruelty of the existing order, serves only to alienate further the individual. At the same time, both Selina Davis and Inez Best feel compelled to do so and their sacrifice is conveyed in Biblical terms.

In the opening of "Let Them Call It Jazz," Selina's homelessness parallels that of the Wandering Jew. "If nobody see and bear witness for me, how to prove anything? So I pack up and leave" (158). The next "home" is no better, for here too there is no one to bear witness, no one to offer salvation. Inez, too, rejects the English in Biblical terms. Upon reading some "English novels about the respectable and the respected" (202), she "reddened with anger" thinking, "*Why, it's not a bit like that. My Lord, what liars these people are! And nobody to stand up and tell them so. Yah, Judas! Thinks it's the truth! You're telling me*" (201). Later, when she defends the suicidal Mrs. Murphy, Inez bears witness for someone in the way that Selina wishes someone would for *her*. But Selina is the ultimate outsider and has only herself. And, indeed, for all that Inez speaks for Mrs. Murphy, nothing is changed by her doing so, for as Selina puts it, "no walls would fall so soon" (175). Madame Tavernier's gift cannot save Inez. The Holloway song lasts only moments and no prison walls fall before it. The machine runs on.

Both stories end with a gift of money to the protagonists, five pounds or a few hundred francs, too little in either case to be of any help to them. Both Inez and Selina remain alone in the face of an English society that is depicted as a mechanized or Biblical hell.

"A Solid House"—England at War

In "A Solid House," Rhys pits one of a long line of "petites femmes" (Teresa) against a pillar of English society (Miss Spearman). One might expect the outcome to be, at the least, explosive. The reverse is true. In a series of exchanges between the two women, nothing untoward occurs, except for the slamming of a single door at the story's end. The narrative has a very steady, almost labored pace, paralleled by the women's movements throughout the house. From cellar to dining room, each venue corresponds to one of five sections which make up the story. Each also corresponds to a block of time from early morning to early evening. The women's conversations are largely superficial in subject matter and polite in tone. Reigning throughout is an air of calm and solidity, supported by the story's predominantly linear organization. Yet there is also a turbulent undercurrent generated by the story's bombed urban setting and by the presence of Teresa, whose guarded manner conceals the fact that she is the antithesis of everything Miss Spearman represents. These two currents (surface calm and underlying turbulence) paint a picture of an inhumane and class-ridden English society and its effects on personal relationships, especially those between women. We see a society not only at war with an outside enemy (the Germans), but deeply and viciously at war with itself.

"A Solid House" begins with Teresa and Miss Spearman sheltering in a cellar during a World War II bomb attack on an unnamed British city. Here are two women sharing a situation of extreme danger, but from the outset their relations are seen to be superficial and guarded, never intimate in any real sense.

> "What's happening now?" Miss Spearman said loudly. She was very deaf.
> "A bit quieter," Teresa shouted.
> Miss Spearman put her hands to her ears and shook her head. She hadn't heard.
> "There, love," she said. Her arms were thin as drumsticks, her chest bony, her hair soft as cat's fur. "It's all over. There, love." (221)

The focus here is Miss Spearman's deafness. As an obstacle to communication, it foreshadows her ideological deafness, which impedes true exchanges. Class attitudes and other differences handicap communication. Teresa's words are variously half-heard, misunderstood, lost altogether, or ignored. A veneer of composed civility covers any resulting confusion (as when Miss Spearman cannot hear Teresa's words, but surmises that the raid is over).

The onus is always on Teresa to try to be understood, never on Miss Spearman to try to understand. Miss Spearman's interest in seances and talking to the dead is ironic in that she shows little interest in communicating with the living. The way in which Teresa defers to Miss Spearman is indicative of the inequality in their relationship. Just as Teresa tells herself, "Don't shout. Pitch your voice right and she'll hear" (223), she is also very careful about *what* she says. While they speak, Teresa reflects, "How much shall I tell her?" (230), and afterward, "How much have I told her? What have I said . . ." (231). Otherwise innocuous exchanges seem as stressful to her as if they were in another language or with a alien culture. Her advice to herself, "Don't shout" (223), is comparable to Selina Davis's intention to speak in a "decent quiet voice" (170) so that people will be sympathetic to what she has to say.

Like a new immigrant to another country, Teresa in Miss Spearman's home must forget herself in order to fit in. She must forget all pain in the past (a failed suicide attempt) and a certain image of herself [represented by a black dress, which, through Miss Spearman, she tries to sell and likens to a "cast-off self" (226)]. She must change the way she speaks as if the flaw were not in Miss Spearman's hearing but in her own speech. She must get used to being alternately scrutinized— " 'Have you been ill?' Miss Spearman asked inquisitively. . . . 'I can see you've been ill. I can see it in your eyes' " (228)—and ignored— Miss Spearman periodically feigns deafness to avoid answering Teresa's questions (228) or when she does not agree with her answers.

> "But I don't like that shade of green. I don't like green at all. It's not my lucky colour."
>
> "What?" Miss Spearman said. "I can't hear you. Take it [the dress] into your room and try it on. A pound to you—and that's giving it away." (226)

Teresa must also silently comply with Miss Spearman's class preju-
dices, never contradicting the older woman's diatribes against the charwoman Nellie and the entire working class. "The whole trouble," she
insists, "is that they promise things that they don't mean to. It's very
un-English, very" (228). In a time of war, this is a hard accusation
indeed, making working-class people seem almost an enemy within.
Miss Spearman's hostility toward the working class is all the more
striking because her own position within the social hierarchy is far from
assured. She does not in fact own the house, but only runs it for the
owner, who has escaped to the Lake District. Teresa reflects that she
looks like "an ex-lady's maid, or housekeeper, perhaps, or poor relation
or half-acknowledged relation—there must be some half-acknowledged
relations knocking around, even in this holy and blessed isle" (223).
However, for the moment Miss Spearman has power and authority,
and Teresa must accommodate herself to that. In fact, on one occasion,
Teresa remarks, "Miss Spearman, I admire you so much" (228). She
goes on to explain, "I admire you because you're always so calm, so
sure of yourself, and because . . ." (228). It is risky to guess what the
unfinished utterance could be, but not too far-fetched to suggest the
word "English." Since Miss Spearman has just condemned the working
class, represented by Nellie, for being "very un-English, very," prais-
ing Miss Spearman for being very English would be logical and in
keeping with the polarization of servant and mistress.

Teresa's tenuous placement in the hierarchy of the house, which
serves as a microcosm of English society (ironically "this holy and
blessed isle"), lies in the fact that she is neither servant nor mistress
and, unlike Captain Roper, not the usual boarder. "I usually let my
rooms to officers," explains Miss Spearman. "But this happened to be
a slack time" (231). But what happens when the time is not "slack"?
Would Teresa's fate be the same as that of Selina Davis, who, after
paying her rent regularly for months, is evicted at the height of the
summer tourist season (158)? The risks of Teresa's uncertain position
are alluded to in the opening of "A Solid House." After the air raid,
Teresa offers Miss Spearman a cigarette.

> But when she opened her cigarette case it was empty. That was
> because the tobacconist on the corner had refused to sell her any
> the evening before. He always refused women customers when there
> was a shortage—and very pleased he was to be able to do it. She
> wondered what the old beast would say if he knew that she rather

liked him. His open hatred and contempt were a relief from the secret hatreds that hissed from between the lines of newspapers or the covers of books, or peeped from sly smiling eyes. A woman? Yes, a woman. A woman must, a woman shall or a woman will. (221)

Although Teresa may say she admires Miss Spearman, at no time does she even admit to liking her. But she "rather liked" the tobacconist who is "open" about his "hatred and contempt" for her (221). She goes as far as saying that his openness is "a relief" compared to "the secret hatreds" that she endures (221). Rhys's lack of specificity (whose "sly smiling eyes"?) adds to an atmosphere of uncertainty and danger. Although Miss Spearman soothes, "There, love," during the raid, Teresa recalls childhood games in which friends turn into bullies. The memory is significant because it points, first, to the possible treachery of one's companions and, second, to their power to accept and then reject their victims. These childhood games reflect Miss Spearman's relationship with Teresa and by extension that of those who have power in society with those whom they neither fully accept nor trust.

The game "started well. You picked your side (I pick you, I pick you), then suddenly, in the middle, something happened" (222). What happens is that the boys decide the girls "aren't officers" and shouldn't participate in the game on the same terms as the boys. The girls will not be as well armed, they will lose, and they will take all the blame for the damage afterward. The German raid accounts less for this memory of a childhood war game than may be at first assumed. To begin with, the war outside the cellar, unlike the children's game, is one with an overt and recognizable enemy. Next, the memory is in fact spurred not by the German bombs, but by the cellar itself. "She remembered playing hide-and-seek in a cellar very like this one long ago" (222).

The boys' power to select or reject the girls is comparable to Miss Spearman's power to rent or not to Teresa. In another parallel to Teresa's childhood memory, we learn later in the story that Miss Spearman usually only let "rooms to officers" and is only making an exception in Teresa's case because it is a "slack time." Other references to Miss Spearman's seeming masculinity and Teresa's female vulnerability suggest a war more treacherous than that of the air raids or of childhood games. Miss Spearman's name is a twofold allusion to her quasi-maleness, in its phallic "spear" and its "man" suffix. Teresa's name, on the other hand, is unmistakably female, or even feminine, with its associations with St. Theresa. The additional link of Christian sacrifice with female suffering is also worth noting. Contrasted with the suggestion of Teresa's vulnerability is that of Miss Spearman's being armed. This again aligns her with the boys in Teresa's childhood, her "spear" being like the boys' knives, which all but the leader of the girls are denied, thus underarming the girls and making their defeat a certainty (222–23).

While Rhys does not give obviously male physical characteristics, her description of Miss Spearman points to an incongruity of sex and gender. In a manner reminiscent of Miss Bruce in "Illusion," who is thin with "large bones and hands" (1), Miss Spearman is thin, but has hands disturbingly unlike the rest of her. She "clasped and unclasped her hands in her lap. They were very red and raw, the joints swollen— the only ungraceful things about her" (228). Her hands are not only large and mannish but somewhat inhuman, their action as they clasp and unclasp recalling claws. The conjunction of her clawlike, masculine hands with her diatribe against her charwoman and the working class in general reveals more than an incongruity in physical appearance. It points to an incongruity in her character.

Like her "ungraceful," even inhuman-looking hands, Miss Spearman's remarks reveal a crude inhumanity which contradicts her appearance of polite gentility. This is evident in the scene after the raid, when she and Teresa are taking tea in the kitchen. Miss Spearman's inhumanity is most striking when she talks about the war. Like the English patients in "Outside the Machine" who chatter about the weather, Miss Spearman talks about life and death with a detached superficiality. "She lit the fire, talking about air raids, land mines and slaughter" (224). The effect of listing "air raids, land mines and slaughter" lulls the reader with a sense of trivializing detachment echoing Miss Spearman's own. The brevity of the list, however, also has the effect of shocking the reader with the speaker's inhumanity. Here Rhys could perhaps be undertaking a study of the dehumanizing effects of modern war on otherwise compassionate human beings, but nothing in the story suggests that Miss Spearman's attitude has ever been otherwise. She is like the square outside the house, which is as "calm and indifferent" during the raid as after it (222).

Miss Spearman's manner is strikingly like that of the only male character, Teresa's fellow lodger, Captain Roper. He sees war in an equally superficial way, the cost of war superseded in importance in his eyes by the diminishing of his masculine image. In a setting comparable in its surface warmth and gentility to that of Miss Spearman's kitchen, Teresa and Captain Roper sit in the drawing room in two fireside chairs. "Battle dress doesn't do justice to a man's figure," he tells Teresa, thus reducing the human cost of World War I to the loss of male status or superiority. The thirties and the Depression are similarly trivialized: "Pop went everything except my dress suit," the Captain complains (224). Here Rhys gives a male character what is traditionally seen as a female characteristic, an excessive preoccupation with fashion, in order to draw attention to English middle-class concerns with image, money, and position. Elsewhere, when Teresa says she admires Miss Spearman and the latter assumes her good looks are being praised, Rhys is pointing less to the older woman's vanity than to her affinity with Captain Roper's worldview.

While Teresa is painfully *self*-conscious, both Miss Spearman and Captain Roper are *class*-conscious. Teresa regards people in human terms, whereas Miss Spearman and Captain Roper (like officers of a rigid hierarchy) regard people in terms of appearance and position in society. Teresa's concerns about humanity transcend any specific class or culture. "Do you think young people are heartless?" she asks Miss Spearman. "Aren't old people heartless? And people who are getting old—aren't they heartless too?" (228). But for Miss Spearman and Captain Roper specifically middle-class, English class concerns outweigh all other matters.

Teresa's remembrance of her second, and last, disastrous evening with Captain Roper shows the incompatibility of these two approaches to life. Captain Roper tells Teresa about a mah-jongg student of his from nearly two decades earlier. "The prettiest woman I've ever seen," he says, but then finds he has forgotten her name.

> "I can't remember her name. A double-barrelled name. It's on the tip of my tongue."
> Double-barrelled names raced through Teresa's brain.
> "Ah, I've remembered it," Captain Roper said. "Barton-Lumley."
> "Barton-Lumley?"
> "Yes, Mrs Barton-Lumley. She got bored," he muttered, and after a pause, "She died."
> Then Teresa had laughed loudly. One of those terrible laughs which now shook her at the most unexpected moments. It came from the depths of her—a real devil of a laugh. Every time this happened she would think, "Who's that laughing?"

> She smoothed her face and tried to turn it into a cough.
>
> "Oh, what a shame! Beautiful people oughtn't to die; they ought to be guarded and protected and kept alive, whoever else dies. There are so few of them."
>
> But this was useless. He looked at her with distrust—and he had gone on looking at her with distrust. (225)

Captain Roper's preoccupation with social class is evident in his fixation with names, here a double-barrelled one instantly identifying the woman in question as a member of the upper classes. Once he remembers it, he has little more to say about the woman. Her name conveys all anyone need know—she had breeding, background, prestige, money (presumably), and a fine future ahead of her. The fact that she died should, in his view of the world, be seen as a tragedy. But his recounting of her fate ("Mrs Barton-Lumley. She got bored. . . . She died") is bathetic. And when Teresa laughs, it is with all the gusto of Selina Davis, and all the abandon of someone who does not fit in. As a result, Captain Roper "looked at her with distrust—and he had gone on looking at her with distrust."

Teresa's faux pas is twofold. First, she laughs at a member of the upper classes. While it is perfectly acceptable to heap insults on working-class figures like the charwoman, another standard obviously applies to the socially superior. Teresa's laugh, which "shook her," also metaphorically shakes the foundation of English society—deference to the class structure. Also, in this instant, she stops deferring to Captain Roper's manhood. She shakes up the order determined by their sex and observable even in their seating arrangements—"he in the big armchair, she in the smaller one" (224). If, as a consequence of her reaction, Captain Roper eyes her with distrust, it is perhaps not surprising. Her actions are comparable to those of a saboteur with regard to the order of things which he, like Miss Spearman, reveres. (Captain Roper's reverence for the social order is, like Miss Spearman's, also all the more striking in that he himself maintains a rather tenuous position within it. Despite his age, he is no more than a captain; and he has in the past been reduced to teaching mah-jongg for a living.)

The second faux pas which Teresa commits is that of letting down her guard. The laughter which "came from the depths of her" is an instinctive reaction, neither tempered nor repressed like so many of her other feelings. In contrast to her controlled, almost stilted words—"Beautiful people oughtn't to die"—her laughter is so uncontrollable it seems to have a will of its own. "Who's that laughing?" she thinks, because laughing at this moment contradicts and undermines all her efforts to control or suppress her thoughts in order to conform to the standards of English middle-class society represented by Captain Roper and Miss Spearman.

More perhaps than any other of Rhys's protagonists, Teresa longs to belong. Inwardly she cries out to the solid, respectable folk who surround her in the solid, respectable house.

> But are you telling me the real secret, how to be exactly like every-body else? Tell me, for I am sure you know. If it means being deaf, then I'll be deaf. And if it means being blind, then I'll be blind. I'm afraid of that road, Miss Spearman—the one that leads to mad-ness and death, they say. That's not true. It's longer than that. But it's a terrible road to put your feet on, and I'm not strong enough; let somebody else try it. I want to go back. Tell me how to get back; tell me what to do and I'll do it. (231)

The self-consciousness that accompanies her words and actions, com-mon to Rhys's "petite femmes," for whom the most ordinary tasks pose extraordinary difficulties, is a symptom of her fear of rejection. For beneath the veneer of a civilized English routine, the tea drinking with Miss Spearman, the fireside chat with Captain Roper, lies a mine-field in which the wrong step can have terrible consequences. Some misplaced laughter (225) or a declined invitation (325) is as damaging as any direct confrontation, which of course Teresa has been trying continuously to avoid.

After Teresa says no to Miss Spearman's invitation to attend a seance, Miss Spearman's words are polite, but as she puts away the dishes, "her friendliness seemed to float away" and she slams the door "so violently" that one is left in no doubt about her feelings toward Teresa. Teresa has alienated herself, even further than before, from her only companion. However peaceful the atmosphere may appear after Miss Spearman leaves, Teresa's isolation, though it may be preferable, is also undeniable and complete. Her repose at the story's end resembles the repose of the dead, an escape from the world of the living. "My little doze," she calls it, and also "My little sleep" (235). Its similarity to the sleep that the nuns call "the little death" (*Voyage in the Dark*, 48) arises from the linking of sleep with escape or peace and death.

In the world created by Rhys in "A Solid House," Teresa's past attempt at suicide seems to suggest that the dead are better off than the living. This view is echoed frequently in Rhys's writing (by Murphy in "Outside the Machine," for example) and may contribute to some critics' perception of her writing as advocating a pernicious passivity. Often, it is alleged, her female characters' suffering does not seem to warrant their extreme sentiments, and they are spinelessly failing to face up to the pressures of life.[18] It would be more accurate, however, to argue that Rhys is pointing at such moments to the lack of choice or place for characters such as Teresa. Following her failed suicide attempt, Teresa still does not feel as if she is alive although she is among the living.

> When you start, you often look back to catch them laughing or making faces in the bright lights away from the fog. Later on you don't do that; you don't care any longer. If they were to laugh until their mouths met at the back and the tops of their heads fell off like some loathsome over-ripe fruit—as they doubtless will one day—you wouldn't turn your head to see the horrible but comic sight. . . . (230)

Her lack of belonging, as she feels it, to humanity as a whole is a magnification of her lack of place in English society. In wartime, a move to continental Europe (an option for many Rhys heroines) is not possible. There is the England, "this holy and blessed isle" (223), inhabited by Miss Spearman or Captain Roper, or there is death, of which the air raids are a regular reminder.

Given that the cellar of the solid house is a place of refuge from German bombs, Teresa's reluctance to leave it once the danger is past may seem curious. She reflects, "She had got used to the cellar, she did not want to leave it now. Why leave this good, this perfectly safe, windowless cellar, so like that other long ago?" (222). "Long ago" seems at first to suggest the childhood games she played in another cellar. But these games were neither "good" nor "safe," but threatening. Throughout the text these games are also linked to events upstairs in the main body of the house—class and gender power. "That other long ago" thus seems to predate both Teresa's present life in Miss Spearman's house and her childhood. By its appearance and the sense of safety it conveys, the cellar is surely one of Rhys's recurrent womb images. Teresa's reluctance to leave is based on bitter experience. Life is precarious and people predatory. Following her brush with death during the raid, Teresa emerges from the cellar as if she were starting her life again.

Like the new model in "Mannequin," whose initiation into the world of Madame Veron's fashion house follows her passage through many rooms and through many obstacles and conflicts within a similar time frame (morning to evening), Teresa pursues her attempt to belong in her ascent from the cellar up through Miss Spearman's solid house. But whereas Anna in "Mannequin" learns to play the "jeune fille" and attains the happiness of belonging, Teresa never reaches her ideal. In fact, she is further from it at the story's end than at its beginning. A crucial difference between the situation of the two protagonists is that Anna is asked to play a role closely resembling herself. Teresa would have to make herself into her antithesis in order to fit in and shows an increasing reluctance to do so. In the following exchange, Miss Spearman sets out the requisite criteria for belonging.

> "Calm?" she said. "Of course, it's better to be calm. I don't believe in hysteria. Not for women, anyhow. Sometimes a man can get away with hysteria, but not a woman. And then of course don't be too much alone. People don't like it. The things they say if you're alone! You had to have a good deal of money to get away with that. And keep up with your friends. Write letters. And a good laugh always helps, of course."
> "Which helps most—with or at?"
> "I don't quite follow you," Miss Spearman said. "And then a little bit of gossip." (231)

The word "calm" is frequently applied to Miss Spearman, just as "shaky" is applied to Teresa, clearly indicating their opposition to one another. Calm, detachment, a sense of superiority, and solidity (like the house, like undefeated England), all these characterize Miss Spearman and are the necessary qualities of middle-class belonging. Teresa lacks all of them. She, emotional, deferential, attempting to reconstruct her life after a suicide attempt, is seen, by comparison, as too female and un-English. Like bombed-out houses and occupied countries, Teresa is from outside Miss Spearman's world and remains so, in one of Rhys's sharpest indictments of the standards and conformity of middle-class English society.

"I Spy a Stranger"—Loose Talk on the Home Front

Join the noble and gallant army of witch-hunters—both sexes, all
ages eligible—so eagerly tracking down some poor devil, snouts
to the ground. Watch the witch-hunting, witch-pricking ancestor
peeping out of those close-set Nordic baby-blues. ("A Solid House,"
231)

Gossip rears its ugly head time and time again in Rhys's fiction. In
its many forms, it is a striking constant in the diverse worlds she creates.
Regardless of the physical setting (continental Europe, Britain, or the
Caribbean) and the time period (the mid–nineteenth-century *Wide Sargasso Sea* to the mid-twentieth-century, almost timeless last stories),
characters in her fiction are as likely to engage in gossip as her protagonists are likely to be its victims. The causes of this victimization by
gossip are quite simple and have less to do with moral standing than
with the chances of one's birth—nationality, race, class position, and
gender. These factors, along with personal choices, such as to live
abroad, to dress in a particular way, and to speak or behave differently
from others, contribute to the profile of a victim of gossip. In essence,
to be anything outside the norm is to invite talk.

It follows that gossiping is purely the pleasure of the insider. By its
very nature, it requires a coconspirator or listening ear. Rhys's protagonists rarely have the luxury of anyone with whom they feel safe to
speak. This accounts for so many hidden monologues, unspoken
thoughts, and incomplete utterances. Conversely, it explains the number of outbursts and bouts of cursing that occur when the burden of
silence becomes too much to bear, for example for Selina Davis in
"Let Them Call It Jazz" and for Inez Best in "Outside the Machine."
Although the message conveyed in these explosive moments is often
the truth, as opposed to the lies and distortions spread by gossips, the
form it takes obstructs the communication of that truth. As a consequence, Rhys's fictional world is like a Godless universe, a world in
which there is no one to hear, "nobody [to] see and bear witness for"
her protagonists' suffering ("Let Them Call It Jazz," 158).

This is the case in "I Spy a Stranger," where a woman is hounded
from her home when the gossip about her spirals out of control.[19] "She
hadn't been here a week before they started making remarks about

her, poor Laura," Mrs. Hudson tells her sister (242). "They didn't stop at nasty remarks either," she continues later (242). Against the backdrop of the Second World War, this chronicle of persecution inevitably draws parallels with events in Europe. While Rhys never directly mentions the persecution and destruction of the European Jews, Laura does refer to "the real horror," as opposed to her own treatment (savage enough in all conscience) (244), and she writes in her notebook: "Why do people so expert in mental torture pretend blandly that it doesn't exist? Some of their glib explanations and excuses are very familiar. I often think there are many parallels to be drawn between—" (249). Laura also contemplates, with some distaste, "the world dominated by Nordics, German version—what a catastrophe. But if it were dominated by Anglo-Saxons, wouldn't that be a catastrophe too?" (248). Moreover the eventual expulsion of Laura from her cousin's house and from the provincial English town is comparable to an act of "ethnic cleansing" (to use the late twentieth century's own distinctive contribution to the language of inhumanity). A letter sent to Laura's cousin voices the xenophobia of her neighbors.

> People in this town are not such fools as you think and unless you get rid of that crazy old foreigner, that witch of Prague, who *you say* is a relative, steps will be taken which you will not like. This is a friendly warning but a good many of us are keeping an eye on her and if you allow her to stay. . . .
> This time next year. . . .
> You'll be all very much the worse for wear. . . . (242–3)

The community does not only gossip; it tells jokes too—jokes that an outsider can only find far from amusing. The attitude of Laura's cousin's husband Ricky is so similarly devoid of human compassion for the protagonist that he also more clearly resembles the enemy than any ally. Not only does he use the word "refugee" as a term of ridicule and contempt toward Laura [" 'These refugees!' he'd say, 'all dressed up and nowhere to go' " (252)], he also jokes about the Gestapo. This he does although he knows Laura has been trying desperately, and without success, to trace her missing friends. Laura's cousin recounts the incident as follows:

> One day when he made a joke about the Gestapo getting her sweetheart she went so white I thought she'd faint. Then she took to

65

staying in her room for hours on end and he didn't like it. "The old girl's got no sense of humour at all, has she?" he said. "And she's not very sociable. What on earth does she do with herself?" "She's probably reading," I said. Because she used to take in lots of papers—dailies and weeklies and so on—and she *hung* about the bookshops and the library, and twice she sent up to London for books. "She was always the brainy one of her family." "Brainy?" he said. "That's one word for it." (246)

As the diminutive of his name indicates, Ricky is juvenile in his behavior. However this does not make him any less cruel. If we ignore his bad taste for the moment (admittedly a rather difficult thing to do), we can see that his joke fails "to laugh her out of it" because it is not "for" Laura, but at her expense. His expecting her to laugh is comparable to the attitude of the painters in "Till September Petronella," who tell the models to "look gay" in order to make a good picture. Lacking any genuine concern for Laura, Ricky expects her at least to put up a good front and to "behave like other people"—meaning good, normal English people (246). Her failure to laugh not only marks her as humorless, but also supports the town gossips' suspicions that she is a foreigner.

Laura is a representative Rhys outsider in her difference from the community that surrounds her. First, she lacks everyone else's sense of detachment toward the war. "She worried so dreadfully about the war," her cousin says later. "You'd have thought she was personally responsible for the whole thing" (245). Second, her sense of attachment to "foreign things," shown by her worries and talk about the war, her efforts to learn the whereabouts of friends, and her consequent decline when she fails, is mirrored by her equally fervent detachment from English things, principally from English manners and conduct.

At least three of her flaws (Ricky regards her as humorless, antisocial, and intellectual) might matter less were it not for her lack of deference. This strikes at the very foundation of English society—its class system and hierarchy. In her refusal to laugh on cue, Laura's disregard for the mores of the English middle class and her placing these below broader concerns of humanity and genuine good taste are laid bare. Her response is not merely a matter of a European preoccupation which overrides Laura's English sensibilities, but of an instinctive sense of compassion, which her reaction to two other jokes also demonstrates.

Here Laura's cousin describes her confrontation with a dinner guest.

. . . it was her own fault. She got people against her. She behaved
so unwisely. That quarrel with Fluting need never have happened.
You see, my dear, he was dining here and he said some of the Waafs
up at the Station smelt. And he was sarcastic about their laundry
allowance. "Pah!" he said. Just like that—"Pah!" . . . But she flew
at him. She said, "Sir, they smell; you stink." He couldn't believe
his ears. "I *beg* your pardon?"—you know that voice of his. She said,
"Inverted commas." He gave her *such* a look. I thought, "You've
made an enemy, my girl." (244–5)

Although Laura's cousin concedes that Fluting was unusually tactless
and badly behaved ("*Most* uncalled for, I thought, especially from a
man in his position"), she favors doing nothing to combat such behavior. "Smile and change the subject, that's all you can do," she insists.
In fact, she partly blames Laura for the unpleasant incident: her lack
of deference to a male opinion, and that of a social superior to boot,
has provoked the quarrel. "It's better not to answer them. Believe me,
it's a mistake," urges Mrs. Hudson (245).

In the third incident of this kind, when Laura once again fails to
see the humor of an insensitive joke, she quarrels with a neighbor
fondly referred to by her cousin as "old Mr. Roberts next door" (250).

You can't imagine why. Because his dog is called Brontë and he
kicks it—well, pretends to kick it. "Here's Emily Brontë or my pet
aversion," he says, and then he pretends to kick it. It's only a joke.
But Ricky's right; she has no sense of humour. One day they had
a shouting match over the fence. "Really, Laura," I told her. "You're
making a fool of yourself. What have you got against *him*? He's a
dear old man." She gave me such a strange look. "I don't know
how you can breathe after a lifetime of this," she said. . . . (250–1)

Once again, Mrs. Hudson's is the voice of social conformity, and
Laura's is that of an outraged humanity, failing to see the joke in the
hopelessly vulgar habits of her respectable English surroundings.

In these and other incidents, Laura not only appears to those around
her to be humorless but also emotionally unbalanced. The fact that
she does not know her place socially is further indicative of her lack
of belonging in a house (not her own), a town (also not her own), and
a country and culture (no longer hers after her years abroad). While
she does contribute to her own alienation by speaking her mind much
like the young boy in "The Day They Burned the Books," she is

also caught in the no-win situation of that story's protagonist/narrator. "Heads I win, tails you lose—that was the English" (153) could equally apply to Laura's experiences in "I Spy a Stranger." She dresses either too well or too poorly (252). She is too serious for others' jokes, or too irreverent, for example, toward the air-raid warden (252). She annoys people by her absence—". . . . she's not very sociable . . . What on earth does she do with herself?" (246)—as much as by her presence— "Why should she plant herself on us?" (246). But whereas the young girl in "The Day They Burned the Books" finds, for a time, a neutral ground for friendship and belonging, Laura remains permanently alone and an outsider. Her only relief is in her notebook and the memories associated with the things, "junk" to her cousin, that she lists in a brief passage in her voice, inserted by Rhys against the narrative flow of Mrs. Hudson's account. *"A cork with a face drawn on it, a postcard of the Miraculous Virgin in the Church of St. Julien-le-Pauvre, a china inkstand patterned with violets, a quill pen never used, a ginger jar . . ."* (251). One might contend that this isolation is the very definition of a Rhys protagonist. But Laura, at least, was not always so isolated. In Europe, she had friends, and she had a home. Thus, the focus of "I Spy a Stranger" is less on the character of Laura and more on the condition of the England in which she finds herself. As one might expect from Rhys, it is a searing portrait of a wartime England quite different from the gallant and cozy myths that have enveloped, and at the time did envelope, this historical moment. The English turn out to be frighteningly similar to the Nazi enemies they are pledged to defeat. A jaundiced, revisionist historian of Britain in the Second World War might do worse than to start with Rhys's bitter short story.[20]

In one of Laura's journal entries, she depicts England in terms of mechanization and destruction:

> An unforgiving sky. A mechanical quality about everything and everybody which I found frightening. When I bought a ticket for the Tube, got on a bus, went into a shop, I felt like a cog in a machine in contact with others, not like one human being associating with other human beings. The feeling that I had been drawn into a mechanism which intended to destroy me became an obsession.
>
> I was convinced that coming back to England was the worst thing I could have done, that almost anything else would have been preferable. I was sure that some evil fate was in store for me and longed violently to escape. But I was as powerless as a useless, worn-out or badly-fitting cog. (247)

While Laura's view of London bears a striking resemblance to Inez Best's view of English society in "Outside the Machine," references to warfare, its mechanization, and a plan for exterminating those who do not "fit" provide parallels with events in Europe which are hard to ignore, given the story's wartime setting. In addition, Laura attempts to escape this destruction by, in effect, hiding out in her cousin's house. With "the curtains drawn" and lights low, she tries to conceal herself, however unsuccessfully. In the end, her own family turns her in, as it were. Bowing to the pressure generated by the gossip in the town, they have her committed to an asylum. Described as "a large ugly house with small windows, those on the top two floors barred" and "surrounded by a high wall" (255), it is presided over by a dubious doctor. Any suggestion of concentration camps, however slight, completes a picture of a country turned in on itself, unable to tolerate difference, and turned away from any human compassion. Because she is not insane the asylum's sole purpose is Laura's confinement.

Laura would doubtless make an uncomfortable neighbor, but her treatment is cruel and unnecessary. The gossip that leads to her expulsion is false. A stranger—yes. A spy—no. Perhaps the most disturbing aspect of Laura's persecution is that the worst of it comes from those closest to her, those who know best how false the allegations of spying are. Why then do Mrs. Hudson and Ricky turn Laura out of their home? Why do they collaborate with her accusers? Some answers can be found in the opening lines of "I Spy a Stranger."

> "The downright rudeness I had to put up with," Mrs. Hudson said, "long before there was any cause for it. And the inquisitiveness! She hadn't been here a week before they started making remarks about her, poor Laura. And I had to consider Ricky, hadn't I? They said wasn't his job at the R.A.F. Station supposed to be so very hush-hush, and that he oughtn't to be allowed—" (242)

Under the guise of telling the story of Laura's ordeal, Mrs. Hudson's own feelings of persecution take precedence. Even within this paragraph, Laura, albeit "poor Laura," does not come first, but somewhere in the middle. First, we are told of Mrs. Hudson's own ill-treatment, and last, the repercussions for poor Ricky. Laura is more a cause of discomfort than an object of compassion. For indeed, we can already see Mrs. Hudson beginning to explain why she and Ricky have betrayed a family member to preserve themselves.

For all that the town gossip is aimed at Laura, it quickly comes to include anyone associated with her. For example, following a shouting match between Laura and an air-raid warden, Mrs. Hudson encounters this reception in, appropriately enough, a butcher's shop.

> . . . I knew it had got round already—I knew it by the way people looked at me. One woman—I couldn't see who—said "That horrible creature ought to be shot." And somebody else said "Yes, and the ones who back her up ought to be shot too; it's a shame. Shooting's too good for them." (253)

Although Mrs. Hudson holds her "head up" on this occasion, after the police descend on the house and confiscate Laura's notebook and letters, any loyalty she has toward her cousin is stretched beyond endurance. The wheels are set in motion for Laura's betrayal. A doctor is called, then a taxi to take her to the sanatorium. The scene in which she is thrown out of her cousin's house is remarkably violent.

> "Come along, old girl," Ricky said. "It's moving day." He put his hand on her arm and gave her a tug. That was a mistake—he shouldn't have done that. It was when he touched her that she started to scream at the top of her voice. And swear—oh my dear, it was awful. He got nasty, too. He dragged her along and she clung to the banisters and shrieked and cursed. He hit her, and kicked her, and she kept on cursing—oh, I've *never* heard such curses. (254)

The potential for violence within good, middle-class English people, revealed earlier in gossip and jokes about the Gestapo, is fully realized here. Instead of intervening, as she knows she should, Mrs. Hudson can only laugh, although her laughter and the sight of Ricky and Laura fighting leads her to conclude, "Something has gone terribly wrong. I believe we're all possessed by the Devil." Her thought may apply not just to her family, but to the whole community and the wartime England it represents.

In the garden, Laura is suddenly calm, her fury turned to quiet disbelief at the course of events: "She stood there . . . talking away—something about how they couldn't do it, that it wouldn't happen. 'Not while there are roses,' she said two or three times" (254). The scene in the garden is richly suggestive. It is the Garden of Gethsemane; it is England (the rose is England's national flower). But what strikes one above all is the calm, the banality, the veneer of civilization that shrouds a scene of betrayal and expulsion. Two women wait for a taxi in a garden, casually chatting about roses. Mrs. Hudson's final words to Laura—"The taxi's waiting, dear"—and Laura's getting into the taxi "without any fuss at all" are frightening in their ordinariness.

If Mrs. Hudson thought that the fight between Laura and Ricky was somehow the Devil's work, what happens in the garden seems worse still. The existence of a devil might imply that of a god. But in the garden, there is only one person's unwitnessed suffering at the hands of another. Indeed, the wicked prosper in Rhys's world, as always. Laura's loss is her cousin's gain. The outsider is pushed out to the point of invisibility behind the sanatorium walls. Mrs. Hudson and Ricky are secure in their own sense of place and belonging and in their status as insiders. The "holy and blessed isle" has been saved.

The Colonies

"The Day They Burned the Books"—"My friend Eddie"

"My friend Eddie . . ." begins "The Day They Burned the Books," and with these three words Rhys sets this story apart from all her others. While it shares the concerns of many of her works—the abuses of power, alienation, class, race, the English, etc.—its starting point remains the focus to the end. "The Day They Burned the Books" is about a friendship, albeit what may be a short-lived one ["People said that he [Eddie] had consumption and wasn't long for this world" (151)], but a friendship nonetheless, and a happy one at that. It may seem paradoxical then that alongside this positive portrait of a friendship, there is a portrait of an abusive marriage, that of Eddie's parents. At the same time, however, the two—the friendship and the marriage—are intimately linked, as any discussion of the former will show.

Central to Rhys's portrayal of Eddie is the crushing weight of the past on the present. The past, as represented by Eddie's parents, is made up of two opposing forces which manifest themselves both physically and psychologically in Eddie himself. With his "pale blue eyes and straw-coloured hair," Eddie is "the living image of his [white English] father" (152). But his manner is that of his "coloured" Caribbean mother. He is "often as silent as his mother" and he shares her antipathy to all things English (152–3). Ultimately, the legacy that his parents leave him is one of social illegitimacy, caught as he is between two cultures and belonging completely to neither. The story is certainly about a friendship, but it is also about the racial and national complexities of growing up in a colonial situation.[21]

It comes as no surprise then that the protagonist-narrator and Eddie are friends. She also bears a burdensome legacy, one that closely resembles that of Anna in *Voyage in the Dark*, of Antoinette in *Wide Sargasso Sea*, and indeed that of Rhys herself. Although both her parents are white, she is island-born and knows of England only through books. As a consequence, she suffers the taunts of the " 'real' English boys and girls" who call her "a horrid colonial" (153). At the same time, she fears "the black children's ridicule" (155).

Any portrait of the friendship between Eddie and the narrator is thus inexorably linked to these legacies, for both characters are outsiders. Whether by looks or ideas, neither the boy nor the girl fit in anywhere but together. The happiness that their friendship provides is, essentially, the happiness of belonging. This is seen in two ways. Especially in the narrator's mind, there is a feeling that they belong "to" one another, much as a husband and wife do. Sometime after the death of Eddie's father, when his mother sets fire to her husband's English books, the two run from the study they had regarded as theirs.

> At his gate he asked me not to go. "Don't go yet, don't go yet."
> We sat under the mango tree and I was holding his hand when he began to cry. Drops fell on my hand like the water from the dripstone in the filter in our yard. Then I began to cry too and when I felt my own tears on my hand I thought, "Now perhaps we're married."
> "Yes, certainly now we're married," I thought. But I didn't say anything. I didn't say a thing until I was sure he had stopped. (156)

The children also feel (both of them this time) they belong to the study, which they come to think of as their own. Described in terms reminiscent of the island's colonization, the children "took possession of the room" after the death of Eddie's father (154). Apart from this invocation of the past in the narrator's use of the word "possession," the study offers a respite from such legacies. Just as no one else enters it "except Mildred to sweep and dust in the mornings," memories of Mr. Sawyer's physical and mental abuse of his wife cease to intrude on their minds. The narrator remarks that "gradually the ghost of Mr. Sawyer pulling Mrs. Sawyer's hair faded, though this took a little time" (154). It is significant that it is only upon the white father's death that the two colonial outsiders can take over his English inner sanctum, full of the symbols of his sense of racial and cultural superiority. But they do, and just as the study provides a respite from the island's heat (entering it "was like stepping into a pool of brown-green water"), so it also provides a temporary escape for the children from the legacies of their births and from their consequent outsider status (154).

As neither the boy nor the girl fits comfortably into the island community, they make this study their own place to belong, and thus remake themselves as insiders. " 'My room,' Eddie called it. 'My books,' he would say, 'my books' " (154). By taking possession of his father's books, Eddie gives himself and the narrator not merely his father's belongings, but a sense of belonging somewhere apart from either the black island community or that descended from the English colonists and colonialists. For although Eddie's mother is "a coloured woman," his resemblance to his English father denies him access to anything but the white community.

His father's status within that community, however, encumbers even that connection.

> His father, Mr. Sawyer, was a strange man. Nobody could make out what he was doing in our part of the world at all. He was not a planter or a doctor or a lawyer or a banker. He didn't keep a store. He wasn't a schoolmaster or a government official. He wasn't—that was the point—a gentleman. We had several resident romantics who had fallen in love with the moon on the Caribees—they were all gentlemen and quite unlike Mr. Sawyer who hadn't an "h" in his composition. Besides, he detested the moon and everything else about the Caribbean and he didn't mind telling you so.
>
> He was agent for a small steamship line which in those days linked up Venezuela and Trinidad with the smaller islands, but he couldn't make much out of that. He must have a private income, people decided, but they never decided why he had chosen to settle in a place he didn't like and to marry a coloured woman. Though a decent, respectable, nicely educated coloured woman, mind you. (151)

Eddie's father does not fit in because he is not the type of Englishman who customarily comes to live in the Caribbean. Twice it is pointed out that he is not "a gentleman." Just as Selina Davis in "Let Them Call It Jazz" is never called by her race but is ridiculed simply for not being white, no name is given to what Mr. Sawyer is, only to what he is not ("a gentleman") and what he lacks ("an 'h' in his composition," the omission of which at the beginning of words has been traditionally seen in England as a sign of lower-class background). His outsider status is evident in the way there appears to be no name for him except in terms of a negation of the expected norm. There is also a suggestion that for the white islanders his presumably working-class background is, like bodily parts, sex, or death, simply too base a thing to mention outright. This origin, coupled with his marriage to "a coloured woman," breaks the rules and thus destroys any possible bonds he might have with the white community on the island.

Eddie, however, contributes toward his own alienation. In a manner resembling his father's, he speaks his mind:

> "I don't like strawberries," Eddie said on one occasion.
>
> "You *don't like* strawberries?"
>
> "No, and I don't like daffodils either. Dad's always going on about them. He says they lick the flowers here into a cocked hat and I bet that's a lie."
>
> We were all too shocked to say, "You don't know a thing about it." We were so shocked that nobody spoke to him for the rest of the day. But I for one admired him. I also was tired of learning and reciting poems in praise of daffodils. . . . (153)

Eddie's presence is equally disquieting when he says nothing at all.

> It was Eddie with the pale blue eyes and straw-coloured hair—the living image of his father, though often as silent as his mother—who first infected me with doubts about "home," meaning England. He would be so quiet when others who had never seen it—none of us had ever seen it—were talking about its delights, gesticulating freely as we talked—London, the beautiful, rosy-cheeked ladies, the theatres, the shops, the fog, the blazing coal fires in winter, the exotic food (whitebait eaten to the sound of violins), strawberries and cream—the word "strawberries" always spoken with a guttural and throaty sound which we imagined to be the proper English pronunciation. (152–3)

As much for what he does not as does say, Eddie shows up the hypocrisy of the others' passion for an England they have never seen. He lets them go on uninterrupted through their absurd list, until their climactic mock-English pronunciation of "strawberries" exposes the sheer nonsense of their sentiments. His words, when he chooses to speak, are not an emotional outburst or slip of the tongue, as is so often the case with Rhys outsiders. Instead, his pronouncement seems deliberate, and this fuels the suspicion that he *wishes* to separate himself, *wishes* to set himself off as distinct from the others. Clearly, his comments about daffodils are a means of distinguishing himself from his father on a scope that differs from normal childhood behavior. The flowers' seemingly sanctified place in English mentality and literature means that he is also distinguishing himself from the English and their colonial imitators. His earlier silence also sets him apart as it is linked to his mother's silence and to a culture that is not only not English, but also not white.

In contrast to Eddie's remarks, those of the narrator-protagonist back-fire on her. Whereas Eddie's words appear deliberate and measured, the girl's, as they try to rebuff the snubs of the " 'real' English boys and girls," simply respond to those snubs and make her appear ridiculous:

> I had discovered that if I called myself English they would snub me haughtily: "You're not English; you're a horrid colonial." "Well, I don't much want to be English," I would say. "It's much more fun to be French or Spanish or something like that—and, as a matter of fact, I am a bit." Then I was too killingly funny, quite ridiculous. Not only a horrid colonial, but also ridiculous. Heads I win, tails you lose—that was the English. I had thought about all this, and thought hard, but I had never dared to tell anybody what I thought and I realized that Eddie had been very bold. (153)

One gets the impression that, whereas Eddie seeks the response his comments call up, thus distinguishing himself from the others, the narrator is caught unawares. Unlike Eddie, whose boldness reflects feelings of superiority as he prompts his separation from the others, the narrator in her efforts to belong is both insecure and lacking in self-confidence. This is well illustrated in the way she first calls herself English, and then, failing to convince her listeners, calls herself "French or Spanish or something like that," whatever might just win their acceptance. But of course none of it does. Her longing to fit in is comparable to that of Teresa in "A Solid House," who sees belonging not in terms of nationality, but of disability. Since the person who represents the society she seeks acceptance in is morally blind and physically deaf, Teresa thinks to herself:

> But are you telling me the real secret, how to be exactly like every-body else? Tell me, for I am sure you know. If it means being deaf, then I'll be deaf. And if it means being blind, then I'll be blind. I'm afraid of that road, Miss Spearman—the one that leads to mad-ness and to death, they say. That's not true. It's longer than that. But it's a terrible road to put your feet on, and I'm not strong enough; let someone else try it. I want to go back. Tell me how to get back; tell me what to do and I'll do it. (231)

The narrator of "The Day They Burned the Books" lacks Eddie's strength to voice unpopular opinions with confidence and, as a consequence, to survive on her own. Eddie's strength is correlated with qualities that are presented as distinctly not English and not white. "But he was bold," the narrator tells us, "and stronger than you would think. For one thing he never felt the heat; some coldness in his fair skin resisted it. He didn't burn red or brown, he didn't freckle much" (153). Indeed, she notes, "Hot days seemed to make him feel especially energetic" (153). For although Eddie has his father's fairness, he exhibits none of the frailties commonly associated with northern Europeans living in warmer climates. By his manner, once again, he more closely resembles his mother. Indirectly, through her part in his genetic makeup, his mother protects him, fueling his boldness.

The girl, however, has no such protector. Her defenselessness is emphasized by her lack of name in the text. Further, as is frequently the case in Rhys's stories, which abound in inadequate or absent mothers, her mother is barely present. She is referred to only once. This is when the girl tells Eddie that her mother "won't take any notice" of Mrs. Sawyer, whatever the latter says about their taking two books from the library, "because she isn't white" (156). An unspoken uncertainty clings to this statement, however, for Mrs. Sawyer's position as the widow of a white, although less than gentlemanly, Englishman and as the mother of a very English-looking son complicates rules of behavior based solely on race. "I was not at all sure," the protagonist thinks to herself, voicing an uncertainty which could equally apply to herself and her own position in society. Her age—she is twelve when Mr. Sawyer dies—contributes toward her own uncertain position. Neither a child nor an adult, neither English nor black Caribbean, she is unaided by any mother-figure and finds a sense of safety, as well as of belonging, in her friendship with Eddie.

Her need for such a haven is clearly illustrated. In her contacts with both the English or the black Caribbeans she fears ridicule. For example, she and Eddie run wildly away with the books they have salvaged from the fire. But as soon as they enter the street, they are aware that by crossing the boundaries of the garden and house for the street, they have crossed over to another culture to which and in which they do not belong. They try not to draw attention to themselves. "When we got into the street we walked sedately, for we feared the black children's ridicule" (155).

As if it is not enough to teeter on the edge of belonging in either group, there is also the risk that someone will give you a push to one side or the other. Exclusion, rather than inclusion, being the norm of social behavior here as elsewhere in Rhys's fiction, the best one can hope for is not to be noticed at all. This rule of self-preservation is practiced, with varying degrees of success, by many of Rhys's protagonists. Teresa in "A Solid House," for example, says little and keeps most of her thoughts to herself. The narrator in "The Day They Burned the Books" is similarly reticent with regard to her thoughts about the English, unlike Eddie. He is attractive to her because he is "bold" and defiant of the obnoxious colonial children around her. Like the white Antoinette in *Wide Sargasso Sea*, who as a child befriends the black Tia—"fires always lit for her, sharp stones did not hurt her bare feet, I never saw her cry" (23)—she admires Eddie for his strength and power to provide an escape from the uncertainties that mark all her other relationships.

A refuge from both the white and black worlds, in which they live but to which they do not belong, is provided by Eddie's father's library. They take full "possession" of it only after the father's death, but even before that it is a place of relief and escape. The library is not, however, for all its English books, a surrogate England. Apart from the two disappointing volumes which they save from the fire, the only book named in the text is *The Arabian Nights*, the product of a third culture and an escapist fantasy for them. Similarly, the games the two children play are neither English imports nor native to the island, but rather role-plays set outside both England and the Caribbean.

> "Now we'll run twice round the lawn and then you can pretend you're dying of thirst in the desert and that I'm an Arab chieftain bringing you water."
> "You must drink slowly," he would say, "for if you're very thirsty and you drink quickly you die."
> So I learnt the voluptuousness of drinking slowly when you are very thirsty—small mouthful by small mouthful, until the glass of pink, iced Coca-Cola was empty. (153–4)

It is fascinating to note that in their game the children are imitating an almost archetypal fantasy (shades of Rudolf Valentino in *The Sheik*) of the interaction of European and non-European cultures. It is however one in which the power relations of nineteenth- and twentieth-century colonialism are reversed, and the non-European succors the helpless European. But whether reading *The Arabian Nights* or pretending they (or only he?) are Arabs in the desert, the pleasures of their friendship together seem to require a neutral ground distinct from the English or black Caribbean worlds to which, however imperfectly, they are linked. In this way, Rhys shows the power of cultural and racial constraints even as they intrude on children's relationships. The racial tensions of the island literally intrude when the children go to borrow *The Arabian Nights*. Mrs. Sawyer looks in the room and at the children, "and I knew that she hated the room and hated the books" (152). Rhys does this to even more dramatic effect in *Wide Sargasso Sea*, when a petty quarrel explodes into a clash of cultures and races, with irretrievable consequences.

> Then she [Tia] bet me three pennies that I couldn't turn a somersault under water "like you say you can."
> "Of course I can."
> "I never see you do it," she said. "Only talk."
> "Bet you all the money I can," I said.
> But after one somersault I still turned and came up choking. Tia laughed and said that it certainly look like I drown dead that time. Then she picked up the money.
> "I did do it," I said when I could speak, but she shook her head. I hadn't done it good and besides pennies didn't buy much. Why did I look at her like that?
> "Keep them then, you cheating nigger," I said, for I was tired, and the water I had swallowed made me feel sick. "I can get more if I want to."
> That's not what she hear, she said. She hear all we poor like beggar. We ate salt fish—no money for fresh fish. That old house so leaky, you run with calabash to catch water when it rain. Plenty white people in Jamaica. Real white people, they got gold money. They didn't look at us, nobody see them come near us. Old time white people nothing but white nigger now, and black nigger better than white nigger. (24)

The exchange between the boy and the girl at the end of "The Day They Burned the Books" is far more muted and has less devastating effects than Antoinette's quarrel with Tia. Yet social realities similarly intrude on what is in the first instance a private conflict, one over the comparative merits of the children's mothers. Running from the garden, the girl at first is "very happy" because she has saved a book from the flames (155). But fears of "the black children's ridicule" in the street prompts worries about her own mother perhaps punishing her. This leads into an unpleasant and complex exchange with the boy. Eddie, "white as a ghost," dressed in a sailor suit, "his father's sneer" on his face, the very model of European colonial supremacy, knows that his mother will do nothing to him. But—and here Eddie is surely echoing the standard contempt of the European white settler for the native other—Mrs. Sawyer will tell lies about the narrator ("She's an awful liar, he says"). The girl lets slip "My mother won't take any notice of her." To which he asks "Why not? Because she's . . . because she isn't white?" (156). The racial conflicts, the racist attitudes of the island are instantly laid bare in the children's exchange, and the narrator develops them. She is at least partly sure that her mother will pay no attention to Mrs. Sawyer because she is not white. She tries to cover up her insult which is no more than the reality of the racially determined inequality of the two mothers, but it is too late. Although Eddie has, in effect, raised the whole issue, he reacts angrily with "You can go to the devil." Like the serpent in Eden, the racial attitudes of the island creep into their secure paradise and disrupt it. As Adam and Eve become conscious of their nakedness and sinfulness, the children become conscious of their legacy of racial inequality and tension. Indeed, the suggestions of an expulsion from paradise give these pages an almost universal undertone. The library is a place of safety from a cruel world; when the children run away, they flee the Sawyers' garden, expelled by Mrs. Sawyer's angry angel; their reconciliation toward the end takes place beneath a single mango tree (152, 155–6).

But although Rhys universalizes Eddie's and the narrator's experiences with such Biblical allusions, she repeatedly returns to specific issues of race and culture. Indeed, Eddie leaps to his mother's defense in his quarrel with the narrator by placing it precisely in those terms. At first sight, his defense seems childish. "She's prettier than your mother," he tells the narrator (156). But there is substantially more to this than mere childish self-defense. Matters of race, culture, and the inescapable legacy of the island's colonial past weigh down his words, as the rest of the passage shows: "When she's asleep her mouth smiles," Eddie insists, "and she has your curling eyelashes and quantities and quantities and *quantities* of hair." The narrator concedes "truthfully," "Yes. . . . She's prettier than my mother" (156).

An earlier description of Mrs. Sawyer suggests that her beauty has gone since her marriage ["what with one thing and another" (151)]. But following her husband's death and during her "cleansing" of all things English and white from her home, her beauty seems restored. The process is seen by the narrator (although she does not put it in these terms) as one of liberation and of a return not just to beauty, but to her island heritage.

> Mrs. Sawyer did not seem to notice that we were there, but she was breathing free and easy and her hands had got the rhythm of tearing and pitching. She looked beautiful, too—beautiful as the sky outside which was a very dark blue, or the mango tree, long sprays of brown and gold. (155)

The rhythms of her movements, the colors, everything contributes to an image of Mrs. Sawyer's harmony with herself, with nature, and with the island, a harmony which strikingly contrasts with the discord of her relationship with her husband. Even the story's title contributes to one's sense that Mrs. Sawyer's actions, though those of an individual, also belong to those of a larger group. Otherwise, why not call the story "The Day *She* Burned the Books"? Rhys's use of "they" in the title not only serves to link Mrs. Sawyer with the black islanders, but also perhaps links her actions with those of the island's former slave population. Thus, her burning of her husband's books (those hated symbols of an abusive and oppressive colonial Englishness) after his death is an act of rebellion, like the burning of white plantations after the emancipation in the 1830s. The black servant Mildred certainly sympathizes—"half hugely delighted, half shocked, even frightened—with her mistress's savage rage" (154–5). Rhys develops this motif of burning as rebellion to even more dramatic effect in *Wide Sargasso Sea*, in which the black islanders' burning of Antoinette's childhood home foreshadows her own burning of the English house in which her husband has imprisoned her.

If the end of "The Day They Burned the Books" is a moment of triumph for Mrs. Sawyer, for Eddie and the narrator it is one of disappointment and defeat. Mrs. Sawyer's act of rebellion and revenge destroys the site of Eddie's friendship with the narrator and deprives him of whatever patrimony (in the widest sense of the world) he could inherit from his father. "Now I've got to hate you too," he shrieks at his mother. "Now I hate you too" (155). Of the two books that they save from the fire, his (Kipling's *Kim*) is torn and incomplete, and hers

(Maupassant's *Fort comme la mort*) is "in French and seemed dull" (157).[22] The disappointments about the books surely echo other greater disappointments and losses. The loss of the library means that there is now no place where they can escape, where they can belong. Whereas for Mrs. Sawyer the book burning is an act of liberation, for the boy and girl it is just the reverse. Having lost the neutral ground where their friendship could flourish, they are forced to return to a society which is polarized according to race, class, and nationality. One assumes that the friendship will not survive.

Although the girl perceives their shared tears as a consummation of their friendship [" 'Yes, certainly now we're married,' I thought" (156)], the story does not end with the pair together in the garden, but apart and alone, with the disappointment of having salvaged nothing they might have wanted. If it takes "a little time" for "the ghost of Mr. Sawyer pulling Mrs. Sawyer's hair" to fade, the image of Mrs. Sawyer taking her revenge will surely take even longer. For its outcome polarizes the boy and the girl according to the legacies of their births. After they run into the street, the girl's imploring "let's go back . . . let's go back" could easily apply to the past friendship, as well as Eddie's house. Crying together under the mango tree in the garden ["a fine mango tree, which bore prolifically" and "was one of the compensations" of Mrs. Sawyer's marriage (152)], they are surrounded by a ruined Eden. They can never truly "go back." *Their* only compensation, like bitter fruits, is the two books that they save, and neither title augurs well for the future.

"Pioneers, Oh, Pioneers"—The Male as Outsider

> *So soon does one learn the bitter lesson that humanity is never content just to differ from you and let it go at that. Never. They must interfere, actively and grimly, between your thoughts and yourself—with the passionate wish to level up everybody and everything. ("Mixing Cocktails," 37)*

Critics frequently and quite rightly emphasize that men are oppressors in Rhys's fiction.[23] However, the short story "Pioneers, Oh, Pioneers" provides another view which deserves some attention. Here, the protagonist, though male, is indisputably a victim and powerless outsider. Mr. Ramage's responsibility for setting himself apart, rather than diminishing his victim status, makes him an especially tragic figure, resembling, among others, Laura in "I Spy a Stranger." His self-imposed exile, in a bid for peace ["Peace, that's what I'm after" (277)], draws special attention to the society that he rejects. Rhys's picture of a male destroyed by the contradictions of a society polarized in terms of class and race is especially powerful because it does so through a figure of traditional male power and authority, the white male colonialist. In "Pioneers, Oh, Pioneers"—and the irony of the seemingly laudatory title is important here—she echoes her even more complex picture of male entrapment and isolation in *Wide Sargasso Sea*.

"Pioneers, Oh, Pioneers" can be viewed in terms of the world that Ramage tries to leave behind. The short story is "an unsettling glimpse of a divided society in which the white population jealously stands together against the larger black one, whose seemingly friendly docility may be cast aside one day."[24] Yet, no less important than the depiction of a divided society is that of Ramage's divided self and his displacement from society. The original title of the story was "My Dear, Darling Mr. Ramage," and its central focus is Mr. Ramage himself and the last two years of his life on a small West Indian island at the turn of the century. Despite the fact that the third-person narration starts and ends with Rosalie and her childish attachment to Ramage, the bulk of the text deals with his arrival on the island, his marriage to a "coloured woman," his increasing isolation from both white and black society, and his eventual suicide and funeral. Indeed, the final section of the framing narrative seems rather sentimental and, if anything, irrelevant to the bleakly humorous and ambitious depiction of the contradictions of a colonial society that forms the rest of the text.

In many ways, Ramage seems destined to be an insider, a representative powerful and empowered male. Like Conrad's Lord Jim, he seems fundamentally "one of us" rather than an outsider. Strikingly handsome, tall, dressed in tropical whites, he comes from England with money to invest in the small island. He buys an estate on the new Imperial Road, which has been built through the island precisely to attract such as he. The property is called Spanish Castle, a name replete with colonial associations. Similarly the estate nearest his has been recently renamed Twickenham after the London suburb. Mr. Ramage has the makings of a colonial icon. But the story takes a different path from the very beginning (the fact that it begins after his funeral is surely important). Throughout the text Ramage is shown not to belong to the empowered and often male figures of Rhys's fictional world, but rather to that predominantly female group of powerless and ostracized protagonists.

In the first section of the story, for example, numerous parallels are drawn, directly and indirectly, between Ramage and other Rhys characters, between "Pioneers, Oh, Pioneers" and other Rhys short stories.

> As the two girls were walking up yellow-hot Market Street, Irene nudged her sister and said: "Look at her!" They were not far from the market, they could still smell the fish.
>
> When Rosalie turned her head the few white women she saw carried parasols. The black women were barefooted, wore gaily striped turbans and highwaisted dresses. It was still the nineteenth century, November 1899.
>
> "There she goes," said Irene.
>
> And there was Mrs. Menzies, riding up to her house on the Morne for a cool weekend.
>
> "Good morning," Rosalie said, but Mrs. Menzies did not answer. She rode past, clip-clop, clip-clop, in her thick, dark riding habit brought from England ten years before, balancing a large dripping parcel wrapped in flannel on her knee.
>
> "It's ice. She wants her drinks cold," said Rosalie.
>
> "Why can't she have it sent up like everyone else? The black people laugh at her. She ought to be ashamed of herself."
>
> "I don't see why," Rosalie said obstinately.
>
> "Oh, you," Irene jeered. "You like crazy people. You like Jimmy Longa and you like old maman Menzies. You liked Ramage, nasty beastly horrible Ramage." (275)

Rosalie's jeering sister places Ramage within a group, "crazy people," which includes, by direct and indirect reference, two other Rhys characters who are victimized for failing to fit in. Jimmy Longa is one of the protagonists of "Fishy Waters," a later story in the same volume as "Pioneers, Oh, Pioneers." A hard-drinking British workman and socialist, Longa is forced to leave Dominica after accusations of brutality toward a child, accusations based as much on rumor as on verifiable fact, turn people against him. Mrs. Menzies "in her dark riding habit brought from England ten years before" resembles Antoinette's mother in *Wide Sargasso Sea*, who also clings to memories of a more prosperous past and "still rode about every morning not caring that the black people stood about in groups to jeer at her, especially after her riding

clothes grew shabby (they notice clothes, they know about money)"
(18).

In its setting too and its juxtaposition of two contradictory worlds,
the opening of "Pioneers, Oh, Pioneers" recalls that of *Voyage in the
Dark*. In frigid England, Anna Morgan remembers the same Market
Street and its people, sights, and smells: "Sometimes it was as if I
were back there and as if England were a dream. At other times England
was the real thing and out there was a dream, but I could never fit
them together" (8). Nor, of course, can Anna Morgan fit into English
society. The link between Anna and Ramage is only that they are
both ostracized outsiders, but the depiction of Market Street has a
significance that goes beyond mere setting in both texts. In *Voyage in
the Dark*, images of the West Indies and England meet in the mind of
the narrator; in "Pioneers, Oh, Pioneers," the two contrasting worlds
meet physically on Market Street in the form of the black and white
women there. In both texts, a double vision or a divided world foreshadows the two protagonists' inability to fit into or belong to one group or
place. Even the date, November 1899, adds to the sense of uncertainty
and displacement, on the edge, as it were, of two seasons, two years,
and two centuries.

The most striking image of Ramage caught between two cultures
involves his very proper English neighbors, the Eliots, the proprietors
of Twickenham. Mr. and Mrs. Eliot are on the boundary of the two
estates "looking at some young nutmeg trees," and about to take the
tea that their servant has prepared, when Ramage appears in very
questionable form.

> They looked up and saw Ramage coming out from under the trees.
> He was burnt a deep brown, his hair fell to his shoulders, his beard
> to his chest. He was wearing sandals and a leather belt, on one side
> of which hung a cutlass, on the other a large pouch. Nothing else.
> (279)

The incident is on one level very humorous. Stark naked, Ramage
stares at Mrs. Eliot and blurts out, "What an uncomfortable dress—
and how ugly!" With admirable *sang froid*, the lady offers him tea,
whereupon Ramage, who "seemed rather confused," bows as if fully
dressed, apologizes, and withdraws. On another level, the incident
clearly presents a man utterly lost between two cultures. He looks the
savage and acts the gentleman. He is neither white nor black (none of

the black islanders wander around naked). He is playing Adam in the Garden of Eden or the noble savage of European fantasies about the "natives" of tropical regions.[25] His misfortune is that there is no place for him in any real community, nor will his fantasies be allowed to survive by either white or black on the island.

In the events that follow this incident, the rumors, the riot, and Ramage's suicide, the protagonist appears quite powerless, situated as he is on the fringes of both the island's communities. For all the motifs of virility—his tanned nakedness, the decidedly phallic hanging cutlass and "large pouch"—Ramage is no better equipped to fend off his tormentors than are any of Rhys's female protagonists in comparable situations. The rumors continue and are fuelled by such images of Ramage, who, as a consequence, is perceived as both "mad" and "dangerous" (280).

The pattern of gossip surrounding Ramage closely resembles that which follows Laura's arrival in the provincial town of "I Spy a Stranger." The subject of the insider gossip is first regarded as "different," then "crazy," and finally "dangerous." However groundless the claims, the danger presumably posed by Laura is clearly stated—the risk to national security in wartime. The danger posed by Ramage is less clearly defined, but much the same. Crossing, as it seems, the boundaries of race and culture on the island, trying to find peace away from a radically divided world, Ramage, by his interracial marriage and his radically altered appearance, threatens the stability of a society based on clearly observed divisions and norms. As the boundaries of race and culture become blurred—is Ramage a savage or a gentleman?—his sexuality comes into even sharper focus. When Ramage's neighbor expresses concern for his wife and daughter, it is clearly Ramage's nakedness rather than his cutlass which poses a threat.

Ironically, it is Ramage's good looks which first favorably impress people. Whereas Jimmy Longa in "Fishy Waters" and Laura in "I Spy a Stranger" are outcasts in the community almost as soon as they arrive, Ramage, at least partly because of his appearance, does not immediately draw people's animosity. In fact, apart from being judged "very unsociable," Ramage is viewed quite positively in the beginning (276). "Miss Lambton, who had been a fellow passenger from Barbados, reported that he was certainly a gentleman and also a king among men when it came to looks" (276). Initially too the black population welcomes him, ironically because of his very imperial appearance. An "admiring crowd of little Negro boys" follows around this handsome man in his "tropical kit, white suit, red cummerbund, solar topee" (276).

What then goes wrong? What turns the Miss Lambtons away and his other admirers into rock throwers? The rejection of Ramage by the black population on the island is straightforwardly motivated by a sense of justice. Because his wife has not been seen for sometime, a rumor has spread that he has killed her. The rejection of Ramage by white society, however, is dealt with in much greater detail. For all that Ramage's marriage to a "coloured girl" is significant, it is moreover symptomatic of his own turning away from English society. His misfortune is that there is no place for him anywhere else on the island, neither among the black population, who show no sign of wanting him as part of their society, nor within the isolation of his own fantasy. Ramage's motives for his rejection of the society and values that could be his are never given (why does he seek "peace"?), but the consequences of his actions are set out in some detail. Following his marriage, Ramage is regarded as "lost to white society" (279), but in truth, he hardly ever did belong, having rejected every opportunity to belong. He is "very unsociable." "He ignored all invitations to dances, tennis parties and moonlight picnics. He never went to church and was not to be seen at the club" (276). His rejection of the very institutions that support white island society not only sets him apart, but also makes him appear threatening. The latter impression is especially powerful because, unlike Jimmy Longa in "Fishy Waters," Ramage for all his eccentricity appears at first to be the perfect English gentleman.

Indeed, viewing Ramage in relation to other Rhys outsiders is as revealing for what he is not as for what he is. Ramage is *not*:

> a member of the working class, like Jimmy Longa in "Fishy Waters" or Eddie's father in "The Day They Burned the Books";
>
> a drunkard, like Lotus Heath in "The Lotus";
>
> destitute, like Selina Davis in "Let Them Call It Jazz";
>
> openly confrontational, like Inez Best in "Outside the Machine";
>
> self-conscious and deferential, like Teresa in "A Solid House";
>
> old, decrepit, rude, and angry, like Mrs. Verney in "Sleep It Off Lady."

The list could go on. Ramage, at least in the beginning of his stay on the island, is inoffensive and amiable, as willing to sing to a child and play a rubber of whist as talk real estate over a whisky and soda (277).

More than that, however, he initially seems ideally suited to be an insider, one of the empowered. Unlike so many other Rhys protagonists, Ramage appears made to fit in. His choice *not* to is nonsensical to both black and white society, both of which class him as mad for his behavior. White society shuns him, and his only white friend, Dr. Cox, reflects after his death that he was "probably a lunatic" (276). His wife is clearly quite hostile toward him, the servants leave, and the locals throw stones at the house (280–1). When the mob goes to the house, they call him "white zombi" (283). This label, however outlandish, is perhaps quite accurate. In *Wide Sargasso Sea*, a "zombi" is said to be "a dead person who seems to be alive or a living person who is dead" (107). Ramage too walks the peripheries of his divided society's communities, belonging properly to neither. Married to a "coloured" islander and possessing the manners of an English gentleman, he lives in a no-man's land of his own savage fantasy. Ramage, indeed, is trying to belong nowhere, to escape. His only goal, as he tells Dr. Cox, is to find "peace" (277).

The estate on the edge of the Imperial Road at first seems to offer the necessary neutral ground. Like the library for Eddie and his friend in "The Day They Burned the Books," it seems to offer a place of escape from a world Ramage rejects. But, as with Eddie and his friend, the divided and hostile world intrudes, and peace becomes as unattainable as privacy. Although there is little intimacy with anyone, one's life is made public and in the end destroyed. The resulting atmosphere is claustrophobic in the extreme. When Mrs. Ramage goes to visit relatives in Guadeloupe, she steals away so secretly that she fuels rumors of her own murder. Afterward she explains "she didn't want anyone to know her business, and she knew how people talked" (283). The atmosphere, as a character puts it in "Fishy Waters," is "suffocating" (311), or, as Laura says to her cousin in "I Spy a Stranger," "I don't know how you can breathe after a lifetime of this" (251). It is an atmosphere very like that of Miss Spearman's house, the microcosm of English society, in "A Solid House." But whereas Teresa is obsessively aware of people's scrutiny and distrust, Ramage seems blithely unaware of these. Although he clearly states his desire for peace, he is not attuned to the dangers threatening it. Although he has made himself an utter outsider and thereby placed himself in a position of vulnerability, his manner is still that of an empowered insider, both confident and casual.

Dr. Cox visits Ramage after the Eliots report his shocking appearance and conduct. Despite the "unkempt and deserted" appearance of Spanish Castle, despite the absence of servants and despite the hostility of the locals, Dr. Cox concludes "The man's as fit as a fiddle, nothing wrong with him at all" (280–1). Ramage receives Dr. Cox with perfect decorum and dressed like an English gentleman. Dr. Cox immediately assumes this to be a sign of mental stability. With his appearance of calm solidity, of "normality," Ramage appears neither a madman nor someone about to be crushed by the contradictions of his own position. Ramage's female equivalent is Miss Bruce in Rhys's first story in *The Left Bank*, "Illusion." Her manner and attire too are impeccably English, but conceal another, altogether different aspect of her character, an aspect which prevents her fully fitting in. Long before her wardrobe of dresses is discovered, Rhys points to the incongruity in her personality through physical detail. Similarly, before Ramage is discovered naked among the nutmeg trees, she indicates something amiss in him. As Miss Bruce is described as tall and thin with mannish hands, so too Ramage possesses a feminine attribute, his hands "long and slender for such a big man" (277). Whereas Rhys is alluding to a sexual ambiguity in "Illusion," in "Pioneers, Oh, Pioneers," Ramage's hands suggest an incompatibility between his personality and the role his society expects him to play. There is surely a gentleness, a lack of traditional masculinity suggested here. Such a trait is, of course, ill-suited to a colonialist or pioneer. Ramage lacks the necessary aggression, nationalistic arrogance, or missionary zeal. All he is seeking is peace and escape, perhaps from the demands of an otherwise impeccably English exterior. His marriage shows a lack of racial sense, and he exhibits no interest in either English colonial society or making money. Echoing the song he sings to Rosalie, Ramage is a "black sheep" among the English on the island. Declared mad by the English, hated by the black population, denied his fantasy of Edenic savagery, he is left no option but suicide. In him, Rhys extends her gallery of outsiders to include a white European male, as she does elsewhere, most triumphantly and complexly in the seemingly victorious, but damned and lost Rochester figure in *Wide Sargasso Sea*.

"On Not Shooting Sitting Birds"—"Heads I Win, Tails You Lose"

The memory which is assigned [the colonized] is certainly not that of his people. The history which is taught him is not his own. . . . He and his land are nonentities or exist only with reference . . . to what he is not. . . . The books talk to him of a world which in no way reminds him of his own. [26]

Before I came to England I'd read many English novels and I imagined I knew all about the thoughts and tastes of various sorts of English people. I quickly decided that to distract or interest this man I must talk about shooting. ("On Not Shooting Sitting Birds," 329)

"On Not Shooting Sitting Birds" is about a date gone wrong. But Rhys broadens the experience of the protagonist, a young West Indian woman in England, to reflect a wide range of cross-cultural experiences. Such an extension is totally unforced and evolves, quite straightforwardly, from details intrinsic to the narrative of the woman and her date. The young white woman discovers that as a colonial she is, contrary to her expectations, excluded from English culture and society, especially when she tries to ape metropolitan mores, and she undergoes the experiences not of the colonizer, but of the colonized, as she is reduced and rejected by the young Englishman with whom she dines. The story resembles a miniature *Wide Sargasso Sea*.

To begin with, there is, as so often in Rhys's texts, no real intimacy between the two central characters. Although they dine together, with a strong prospect (albeit unfulfilled) of sleeping together, they are and remain utter strangers. She bases all her knowledge of England on English novels; he has no notion of the West Indies "at all" (329). Much as in "A Solid House," where the onus lay on Teresa to compensate for Mrs. Spearman's deafness, the West Indian protagonist/narrator in "On Not Shooting Sitting Birds" tries to compensate for an Englishman's ignorance of her homeland with disastrous results.

"On Not Shooting Sitting Birds" is one of Rhys's shortest stories, and, at the same time, one of her most intricate. It consists, in fact, of three separate narratives, each of which involves an invisible other, a character (the protagonist/narrator) made doubly invisible by being both female and West Indian. The first narrative, and main text, is the protagonist/narrator's remembrance of an ill-spent evening with an

Englishman she barely knows. The second and third narratives are, respectively, the protagonist/narrator's fictional and actual accounts of a West Indian shooting party. In each one the invisible, colonial, female otherness of the protagonist/narrator points to a power and authority possessed by the male character which is as much cultural and national as sexual in its origins.

The main text, for example, entitled as it is, and not, say, "Pink Milanese Silk Underclothes," points immediately to conflicting cultural, not sexual, mores. Initially, however, the reverse appears to be the case. Here the protagonist describes her preparations before her date:

> One day, I've forgotten now where, I met this young man who smiled at me and when we had talked a bit I agreed to have dinner with him in a couple of days' time. I went home excited, for I'd liked him very much and began to plan what I should wear. I had a dress I quite liked, an evening cloak, shoes, stockings, but my underclothes weren't good enough for the occasion, I decided. Next day I went out and bought the milanese silk chemise and drawers. (328–9)

The female speaker is casual, confident, methodical, as she looks ahead to the evening. She seems empowered by her preparations and in no measure shies away from the prospect of a sexual encounter with a virtual stranger. Indeed, she plans for it, buying, as she does, new undergarments specifically for the occasion. The importance of this purchase cannot be overemphasized. The "milanese silk chemise and drawers" are mentioned three times—at the very start of the narrative (the memory of their purchase triggering other recollections), midway through the narrative, and at its end. After the failure of her date with the Englishman, the woman concludes:

> I felt regret when it came to taking off my lovely pink chemise, but I could still think: Some other night perhaps, another sort of man.
> I slept at once. (330)

Earlier, when the protagonist lists what she will wear (from her outermost to her most intimate garments), the "pink milanese silk underclothes" (328) gain a prominence that is intended to give us an understanding of the character of their wearer. The color pink suggests, in contradictory turn, femininity, youth, and innocence (which the protagonist's tone and words also indicate); the flesh (by color and by the underclothes' proximity to it); and sexual arousal. Later these contradictions return. When the Englishman keeps eyeing her "in such a wary, puzzled way," finally asking, "But you're a lady, aren't you?" "exactly as he might have said, 'But you're really a snake or a crocodile, aren't you?' " (329), the seeming contradictions in her character, which her choice of clothes reflects, become unavoidable and impassable. "We looked glumly at each other across the gulf that had yawned between us," she says (329).

What follows, now already halfway through this very short text, are the facts of the cultural differences that not only separate but also polarize these two individuals. The woman is West Indian; the man is English. Whereas she comes from a culture in which people are largely categorized by color, his is a culture based on class. Both are systems for "placing" people, especially the perfect stranger, for fixing who are outsiders and who insiders. Both systems are highly complex. These complexities form a major concern elsewhere in Rhys's fiction. In "Trio," for example, Rhys shows the complexities of color-based classifications, which go beyond mere black and white labels. In a Montparnasse restaurant, the speaker observes three West Indian "compatriots." The man is "very black—coal black," the woman however is "coffee-colored and fat," while the girl "evidently" has "much white blood in her veins" (34). The English system also has its complexity, as Rhys indicates in "Outside the Machine," when Inez asks in an ironical interior monologue, "An English person? English, what sort of English? To which of the seven divisions, sixty-nine subdivisions, and thousand-and-three subdivisions do you belong?" (192). The problem facing the Englishman in "On Not Shooting Sitting Birds" is that his companion defies classification. She is at once a lady *and* a tramp. But the impossibility, as far as he is concerned, that anyone can be both reinforces the perception that she cannot, in effect, exist at all.

Whereas the Englishman appears "stiffer" than when they first met, and also "wary" and "puzzled" (329), the woman is, for the most part, relaxed, unapprehensive, and clear-sighted about the evening ahead. She is the antithesis of the "petite femme" epitomized by Anna in *Voyage in the Dark*, who, shocked to discover her date's sexual expectations, squeals, "Oh . . . it's a bedroom" (20). Yet the two scenarios are virtually identical. Both feature young, white West Indian women dining out at the clubs of upper-class Englishmen whom they know only slightly. But whereas Anna is shocked, the protagonist of the short story anticipates the sexual expectations of the Englishman. Indeed, she plans for it, purchasing her fancy underwear beforehand in a state of unabashed excitement. And whereas Anna is all nerves, on the brink of hysteria, this protagonist's calm is obvious even in her brief description of the scene. "So there we were," she states matter-of-factly, "seated at a table having dinner with a bedroom very obvious in the background" (329).

What the West Indian woman does not foresee is how ill at ease her partner will become in response to her unabashed sexuality. Realizing early on that she is not a tramp, but a lady, the Englishman cannot reconcile the incompatibility, in his view, of two such opposites. When she answers his "But you're a lady, aren't you?" with "Oh no, not that you'd notice," her unconvincing impersonation of a tramp's frivolity fails to bridge the gap between them. Of course, the protagonist is a lady in her own West Indian terms, simply because she is white. The Englishman's question makes so little sense to her that she turns it off as a joke. But because she does not fit his image of women, she can have no belonging or connection to him. Her situation here as a woman is comparable to that of the colonized subject which she also is, remade into a nonentity, invisible, existing only with reference to what she is not (Memmi, 105). Neither a tramp nor truly a lady in the Englishman's limited understanding, she is nameless and as effectively nonexistent as the West Indies, about which he knows nothing.

Failing as a lady and failing as a tramp, the protagonist assumes a role garnered from "English novels" which she believes will "distract or interest" the man (329). In this, the second narrative contained in the story, the protagonist gives fictional accounts of being lost as a child in the Dominican forest and participating in a West Indian shooting party. The first account seems to bear less relation to any reality than to a Grimms' fairy tale—the helpless female child, the threatening forest itself a series of phallic images. Although the narrative gives few details, its bare outline echoes European children's literature and indicates the teller's attempt to bridge the cultural gap between herself, a West Indian, and this European. In truth, she tells the reader, the story is a fabrication. "I'd often been in the woods but never alone" (329). The sense of ease and familiarity that "often" lends to her statement is in keeping with her casual attitude toward sex. "Been,"

rather than, for example, "ventured," demystifies the experience, reducing it to its mundane reality. At the same time, the words "but
never alone" introduce a sense of practicality (one must be careful not
to get lost) that is in keeping with the protagonist's own pragmatism,
as evinced by her preparations for the evening engagement.

The woman prefaces her fictional shooting party story with some
information on the West Indies the man is so ignorant of:

> There are no parrots now . . . or very few. There used to be. There's
> a Dominican parrot in the zoo—have you ever seen it?—a sulky
> bird, very old I think. However, there are plenty of other birds and
> we do have shooting parties. Perdrix are good to eat, but ramiers
> are rather bitter. (329)

Although the Englishman makes no response until much later, near
the end of her account, the dashes and unanswered question above
suggest that she is as good as speaking to herself. Failing to excite his
interest in things West Indian, she attempts again to show how like,
rather than unlike, her homeland is to his England. The stress on
"do"—"and we do have shooting parties"—is one such attempt, as is
her sentence on "perdrix" and "ramiers" which follows. This is a quite
complex sentence in its attempt to conform to Englishness and its utter
failure to do so. First of all, she gets it right, talking about the correct
kinds of birds, and with just the proper English upper middle-class
inflection on "rather bitter." But, of course, she also gets it outrageously
wrong. Instead of partridge, she says "perdrix"; instead of woodpigeon,
"ramiers." The French names are not pretension, but the colonialisms
of an island culture isolated from the motherland and near to Guadeloupe and the French West Indies. Just as with her joke about being
a lady, the woman stumbles as she tries to gain the man's acceptance.
She cannot "pass" as an Englishwoman, for "passing" here is as much
linguistic as behavioral, and she just does not have the right words.

But she continues to try to gain acceptance and goes on with an
utterly fictional account of a shooting party. So divorced is this account
from the real thing that she hardly pays attention to what she is saying
and thinks instead of the reality, which she could not describe in detail
anyway as she always hid from the noise of the guns. Somewhere in
her fictional account (neither she nor the reader knows quite where)
she slips up, and the whole relationship, such as it is, collapses and
she makes herself an un-person, an outcast for the metropolitan En-

glishman: "On and on I went, almost believing what I was saying, when he interrupted me. 'Do you mean to say that your brothers shot sitting birds?' His voice was cold and shocked" (330).

As so often in Rhys's writing, the smallest things matter. Seemingly inconsequential details carry considerable weight for her protagonists. Their mistakes are often the tiniest of slips. For each slipup marks the slippage of the assumed mask, revealing as it falls what the protagonist wishes to conceal. The slip marks their outsider status. Whether it is the revelation of Miss Bruce's secret wardrobe in "Illusion," Teresa's escaping laughter in "A Solid House," or Ramage's nakedness in "Pioneers, Oh, Pioneers," the effect of such mistakes is irreversible. The mask that falls in "On Not Shooting Sitting Birds" is a cultural one. The fictional account of a West Indian shooting party reveals that it bears no relation to an English one. Whether or not the woman's brothers did shoot sitting birds is irrelevant, and she cannot remember one way or the other. What matters is that this is what the Englishman is led to believe and what happens as a consequence of his belief.

The results are threefold. The Englishman is repelled; his relationship with the woman is irreconcilably polarized; and his sense of cultural superiority is bolstered. Thereafter the evening goes from bad to worse. She has become a nonperson to him, no longer someone he wants even a casual sexual encounter with. She is not sure she likes him any more, and after a "most uncomfortable dinner" they part with the most superficial of civilities. The protagonist's very attempt to conform, to belong, results in rejection and contempt. Like the young girl in "The Day They Burned the Books," whose futile attempts to conform to English standards cause her to conclude, "Heads I win, tails you lose—that was the English" (153), this protagonist's efforts leave her worse off than before. One can see the pattern being repeated, which casts a dark shadow over her cheery optimism at the end of the text. "Some other night perhaps, another sort of man" (330). Not, one suspects, in England, for there is nothing to suggest this Englishman is anything out of the ordinary. He is nondescript and, like the woman, nameless. It is no accident that any discussion of the story has to talk of "the Englishman" and "the West Indian woman," for the characters never cross these borders into any state of individuality or intimacy with each other. They remain as isolated from one another as the two islands they represent.

The protagonist, it must be said, is not without blame. It is her choice, after all, to try to impress the Englishman with a fictitious rather than a factual account of a West Indian shooting party. What she conceals is less important than the fact she tries to conceal something at all (only a child at the time of the shooting parties, she was too frightened of the noise of the guns to know whether West Indians do shoot sitting birds). Her act of self-censorship signifies the distrust that a hostile, metropolitan atmosphere breeds. "I had started out in life trusting everyone and now I trusted no one, So I had few acquaintances and no close friends," she says near the beginning of the story (and recalls here a long list of Rhys protagonists both English and West Indian).

If Rhys's works appear unrelentingly dismal at times, it is worth asking how much this arises from the worlds she describes, rather than from the characters who populate them. If the protagonist of "On Not Shooting Sitting Birds" is to be faulted, it is not so much for choosing to censor her past (is not assimilation a form of self-censorship?), but for wasting her efforts on such an unworthy companion and the world he represents. Although many of Rhys's protagonists are difficult and, at times, unlikable, they measure up better than most of the characters around them. Not the least is the figure of the young West Indian woman in this story who against all odds can still say, "I never quite lost the hope of something better or different" (328).

Conclusion

Rhys's protagonists are all outsiders—women, men, old, young, West Indian, English. For her it is a generalized existential state. But outsiderdom does not exist in a political, social, or cultural vacuum. It is historicized and located in specific times, places, and types of social organization. It intersects with and is an aspect of the power of men over women, of those with money and position over those who are marginal, of the English over the stranger, of the colonizer over the colonized, of the white over the black. It is a matter of social class, of race, and of gender. These specific social and economic situations allow no middle ground, no escape, but unremittingly grind down those who for whatever reason cannot fit in. Rhys's vision is almost unrelievedly dark. The only rays of hope lie in the pluck of many of her protagonists and the resistance they offer, however ineffectually, to the forces that confront them.

Notes to Part 1

1. Ford Madox Ford, "Preface: Rive Gauche," *The Left Bank* (London: Jonathan Cape, 1927), 23–4; hereafter cited in text.

2. This is a theme that runs throughout Rhys criticism. See, for example: Conrad Aiken, "Stories Reduced to Essentials," Review of *The Left Bank*, *New York Evening Post*, 1 October 1927, 10; Review of *The Left Bank*, *Spectator*, 30 April 1927, 772; A. Alvarez, "The Best Living English Novelist," *New York Times Book Review*, 17 March 1974, 6–7; Paul Piazza, "The World of Jean Rhys," *Chronicle of Higher Education*, 7 March 1977, 19; Irene Thompson, "The Left Bank Apéritifs of Jean Rhys and Ernest Hemingway," *Georgia Review* 35 (Spring 1981): 94–106; Nancy Hemond Brown, "Aspects of the Short Story: A Comparison of Jean Rhys's 'The Sound of the River' and Ernest Hemingway's 'Hills Like White Elephants'," *Jean Rhys Review* 1 (Fall 1986): 2–12. See also Gregg, 35–6. The comparison is frequently made to Hemingway, and all commentators agree on the pared-down qualities of the style; however, few, apart from Gregg, analyze Rhys's style in any depth.

3. See excerpts from Rhys's letters and from her conversations with David Plante quoted in Part 2 of this book. Interesting material is also available in Veronica Marie Gregg, "Jean Rhys on Herself as a Writer," in *Caribbean*

Women Writers: Essays from the First International Conference, ed. Selwyn R. Cudjoe (Wellesley: Calaloux, 1990), 109–115.

4. See Rhys's letter to Francis Wyndham, 6 December 1960, in *The Letters of Jean Rhys*, ed. Francis Wyndham and Diana Melly (New York: Viking, 1984), 197; hereafter cited in text as *Letters*.

5. See, for example, Paul Bailey, Review of *Tigers Are Better-Looking*, *London Magazine*, June 1968, 111, for a representative comment on Rhys's lack of variety and range.

6. See, for example: Review of *The Left Bank*, *New Republic*, 10 November 1927, 345; "Miss Rhys's Short Stories," Review of *The Left Bank*, *New York Times Book Review*, 11 December 1927, 28–30; D. B. Wyndham-Lewis, "Hinterland of Bohemia," Review of *The Left Bank*, *Saturday Review*, 23 April 1927, 637. See also Morrell, 242.

7. This is one of the predominant themes of Rhys criticism. Gardiner (31) sees inclusion and rejection as the organizing principle of *The Left Bank*, while Howells (33) writes of the "others" who populate this collection. Both Hite (25, 47) and Alvarez (7) comment on the marginality of her central figures, and this is also a major topic of Ford's Preface to *The Left Bank* (24) and of Naipaul's review of *After Leaving Mr. Mackenzie* (29, 31). See also Christine Jordis's comments on *"non-appartenance"* (not belonging) in her essay "Jean Rhys ou la perspective de l'exil," in *La Nouvelle Revue Française* (July–August 1983): 156–67 (156); and Mary Sullivan, "All Underdogs," Review of *Tigers Are Better-Looking*, *Listener*, 25 April 1968, 549.

8. Jean Rhys, *Voyage in the Dark* (New York, London: Norton, 1982), 54. All subsequent references are to this edition and appear in the text.

9. Jean Rhys, *Wide Sargasso Sea* (New York, London: Norton, 1982), 69–70. All subsequent references are to this edition and appear in the text.

10. Emery (3–7) has interesting comments on "masquerade" as a positive force in Rhys's fictional world.

11. This approach permeates Angier's 1990 biography from beginning to end. Gloria Fromm's comments on Rhys and autobiography are interesting in "Making Up Jean Rhys," *New Criterion*, December 1985, 48–9. See also Laura Niesen de Abruna on readings of Rhys's fiction as personal therapy in "Jean Rhys's Feminism: Theory against Practice," *World Literature Written in English* 28, no. 2 (1988): 327–28.

12. Jean Rhys, *Good Morning, Midnight* (Harmondsworth: Penguin, 1969), 111. All subsequent references are to this edition and appear in the text.

13. Jean Rhys, *After Leaving Mr. Mackenzie* (Harmondsworth: Penguin, 1971), 23. All subsequent references are to this edition and appear in the text.

14. The feckless incompetence of Rhys's protagonists is often stressed and judged negatively by critics. See, for example: Piazza, 19; Nancy J. Leigh, "Mirror, Mirror: The Development of Female Identity in Jean Rhys's Fiction," *World Literature Written in English* 25, no. 2 (1985): 271; Linda Bamber, "Jean

Rhys," *Partisan Review* 49 (1982): 93; Julian Jebb, "Sensitive Survivors," Review of *Tigers Are Better-Looking, The Times*, 30 March 1968, 21; Diana Johnson, "Overdrawn at the Left Bank of the World," Review of *Tigers Are Better-Looking*, 3 November 1974, 1.

15. Paula le Gallez has an illuminating chapter on the way in which Fifi is silenced and reduced in the course of the text. See "Reducing Fifi" in Paula le Gallez, *The Rhys Woman* (New York: St. Martin's Press, 1990), 9–21.

16. The topic of Rhys's attitudes toward England and the English is ably discussed in Nancy Hemond Brown, "England and the English in the Works of Jean Rhys," *Jean Rhys Review* 1 (Spring 1987): 8–20. Rhys's letters contain a clear current of hostility toward things English; see, for example, letters to Evelyn Scott, 10 August 1936, and to Peggy Kirkaldy, 4 October 1949 (*Letters*, 32, 56).

17. For a further discussion of these topics in Rhys's fiction see: Isabel Carrera Suárez and Esther Alvarez López, "Social and Personal Selves: Race, Gender and Otherness in Rhys's 'Let Them Call It Jazz' and *Wide Sargasso Sea*," *Dutch Quarterly Review of Anglo-American Letters* 20 (1990–92): 154–62; and Lucy Wilson, " 'Women Must Have Spunks': Jean Rhys's West Indian Outcasts," *Modern Fiction Studies* 32 (Autumn 1986): 439–47.

18. See note 14 above.

19. Howells's comment on "the brutal mechanics of 'othering' " is particularly apt here (144). For a further discussion of this story and "Temps Perdi," see Nancy J. Casey, "The 'Liberated Woman' in Jean Rhys's Later Short Fiction," *Revista Interamericana Review* 4 (Summer 1974): 264–72.

20. Perhaps it is not surprising that Rhys was advised to exclude this story from *Tigers Are Better-Looking* (Angier, 581). However, it had been accepted for publication in *Art and Literature* in 1966 (*Letters*, 295), and was published in *Penguin Modern Stories* in 1969.

21. Rhys's success in writing about colonial situations is discussed by Judith Kegan Gardiner in "The Exhilaration of Exile: Rhys, Stead, and Lessing," in *Women's Writing in Exile*, ed. Mary Lynne Broe and Angela Ingram (Chapel Hill: University of North Carolina Press, 1989), 134–50. Howells is, as always, perceptive on this issue in her analysis of "The Day They Burned the Books" (139–41). Rhys's ability to write acutely about the contradictions of colonial life allows Neville Braybrooke to discuss her as a Caribbean writer in "The Return of Jean Rhys," *Caribbean Quarterly* 16 (December 1970): 43–6; and we have already noted how V. S. Naipaul is prepared to judge her as such (Naipaul, 29–31).

22. *Kim* is, of course, a most appropriate if ironic choice of book for the displaced Eddie. Like him, the hero of Kipling's novel is torn between two cultures, but one feels that Eddie will not find a place within a benign British Empire as his earlier fictional counterpart does. Maupassant's text also concerns a hero who is torn, in this case, between two loves—for a woman and her

daughter: "Et il vivait près d'elles, partagé entre les deux, inquiet, troublé" (And he lived near them, divided between the two, uneasy, troubled) (part 1, ch. 4). Neither woman is wholly attainable, just as the boy and girl in "The Day They Burned the Books" can not wholly attain belonging to any part of the island community. Maupassant's hero's love letters, which he watches burn before he dies, parallel the books in the library in Rhys's story. Metaphors of a brief happiness, their burning foreshadows a dark future. The allusion to the Song of Solomon (8:6) in the title of Maupassant's novel is also quite appropriate to Rhys's story. The Biblical text reads: "Set me as a seal upon thine heart, as a seal upon thine arm: for love is strong as death; jealousy is cruel as the grave: the coals thereof are coals of fire, which hath a most vehement flame." Mrs. Sawyer's jealousy and anger and the fire that burns the books are here. The assertion that "love is strong as death" is, however, ironic in relation to Rhys's story. The girl's and Eddie's love is doomed; the forces of death are much stronger.

23. See, for example: Morrell, 102; Hite, 23–4; Howells, 11–12.

24. Eve Auchinloss, "Lighting Up the Inner Dark," Review of *Sleep It Off, Lady*, *Washington Post Book World*, 7 Nov. 1976, G2.

25. For the reader of Jean Rhys, *Wild Majesty: Encounters with the Caribs from Columbus to the Present Day: An Anthology*, ed. Peter Hulme and Neil L. Whitehead (Oxford: Oxford University Press, 1992), provides interesting examples of European fascination with "noble savages," in this case, with the Caribs of Rhys's native Dominica. Rhys herself writes of the Caribs in an extended section of the story "Temps Perdi," and the section is included in *Wild Majesty*.

26. Albert Memmi, *The Colonizer and the Colonized* (Boston: Beacon Press, 1991), 105; hereafter cited in text.

Part 2

THE WRITER

Introduction

The best source of information on Rhys's views of herself as a writer and as a writer of short stories is *The Letters of Jean Rhys*, edited by Francis Wyndham and Diana Melly. The following section reflects this fact by quoting extensively from them. Her 1979 interview with the *Paris Review*, while certainly of interest, hardly mentions her short stories at all. The other major published source of her views on writing is the record of her conversations with David Plante. Although one must treat these with caution (Plante is transcribing them from memory, one assumes, and cannot give Rhys's *exact* words), nevertheless there is material here that may illuminate Rhys's view of herself as a short-story writer. Whichever the source, Rhys's observations specifically on the short story are quite limited. She sees herself primarily as a novelist, and the short stories are less central to her view of herself as a writer. However, she does make numerous comments on the short stories that make up *Tigers Are Better-Looking*, and these help to form a support for her argument that English publishers and readers are not really prepared for the bitter truths about England and the world that she chooses to reveal. Throughout her comments on the short story and on English attitudes she shows her normal disdain for what she sees as English hypocrisy and indifference to the truth. Her comment, recorded by David Plante, on the short stories in *Sleep It Off Lady* is surprisingly negative. They are "no good, no good, magazine stories." Perhaps this illustrates as well as anything Rhys's self-doubt as a writer, which uncomfortably accompanies her defiant sense of herself as a teller of bitter truths.

Although she may have been assailed by self-doubts, Rhys is meticulous and painstaking in her craftsmanship. Veronica Marie Gregg has documented Rhys's constant revisions of texts in order to achieve particular effects (Gregg, 37–40). Her letters also reveal a writer concerned with the minutiae of her craft, while her conversations with Plante often take the form of one professional talking to another. Cutting unnecessary material and trying to get the precise and appropriate word or phrase were central to her writing habits. Writing was clearly something that she did not find easy. "There is no penny, no slot," she declares. She also insists that she is not concerned about her possible audience. She tries to "blot them out," and the only attempt she made to write a story for purely commercial reasons led to her tearing it up in distaste. This attitude is despite her love and need of money and success.

Recent criticism (for example, by Gayatri Spivak and Coral Howells) has very much emphasized Rhys's position as a colonial, West Indian writer. In her letters, she fleetingly acknowledges the importance of the West Indies in her fiction. For her, in her writing, there are only Paris and Dominica, the places she loves and constantly harks back to. She points out, however, that it is the West Indies of her childhood, now vanished, about which she writes.

Perhaps one of the most vexed issues in Jean Rhys criticism is that of the autobiographical nature of her work. Rhys herself is contradictory on this issue. Toward the end of her life, in her conversations with Plante and in her 1979 interview in *The Paris Review*, Rhys certainly acknowledges a confessional, autobiographical element in her writing. "I can't make things up. I can't invent. I have no imagination. . . . I just write about what happened," she tells Plante. However even here she hesitates. "Not that my books are entirely my life—but almost." Plante also records her insistence that she thought first of the "shape" of a book, and then adapted material from her life to fit that. In fact, the writing only feels good, she declares to him, when she feels she is a pen in the hand of some greater force. Some of her letters, indeed, point to a much less biographical reading of her fiction. In them she expresses a hostility toward personal publicity and an immediate biographical reading of her work. Perhaps we should pay some attention to this argument and acknowledge the conscious artistry of Rhys's writing, instead of seeing Rhys's writing, rather demeaningly, as simply transposed autobiography. As she wrote, tellingly, to Francis Wyndham in 1960, "Only the writing matters."

The following material from Rhys's letters is divided into four sections: her comments on her short stories and on short fiction in general; evidence of her writing habits and of her views on herself as a woman writer; two passages illustrating the centrality of Dominica and the West Indies in her mental world; and her observations on her works as autobiography. The extracts from Plante's book are simply given in the order in which they appear in the original.

Notes on Rhys's Correspondents

Peggy Kirkaldy. Literary socialite in London. An admirer of Rhys's work and long-term friend, she corresponded with Rhys from the 1930s.

Diana Athill. A director of the publisher André Deutsch, a constant supporter of Rhys's later work, editor of *The Collected Short Stories*.

Morchard Bishop (real name, Oliver Stoner). Novelist and biographer, he corresponded with Rhys from the 1930s until her death.

Evelyn Scott. U.S. novelist and prominent intellectual in Greenwich Village in the 1920s. Enthusiastic (if unsuccessful) promoter of Rhys's work in the United States in the 1930s.

Selma Vaz Dias. Actress and painter. Adapter of Rhys's novels for stage and radio. She maintained a sometimes stormy friendship with Rhys beginning in the late 1940s.

Francis Wyndham. Editor. Tireless supporter of Rhys and her work from the 1950s onward.

Maryvonne Moerman. The daughter of Rhys and her first husband, Jean Lenglet. She remained with her father in Holland during World War II and was a member of the Dutch Resistance.

From *The Letters of Jean Rhys*

Short Stories

I've a book of short stories finished but no faith in them. Too bitter—also who wants short stories?

(Letter to Peggy Kirkaldy, October 1945)

I hope to send my book [containing most of the stories printed in *Tigers Are Better-Looking*] to Constable this week—it's been the hardest thing I've ever done in my life—the only advantage of that being that I don't much care what happens to it. Yes I do care, but only because Leslie liked the stories.

(Letter to Peggy Kirkaldy, 11 February 1946)

Peggy—about my book [the stories in *Tigers Are Better-Looking*]—the trouble is—it is not good. Three stories are all right. The others are competent. That's all—I can't try to sell it with passion for I know its faults. I tried too hard for one thing, and was so afraid of offending that I wrote and rewrote the life out of the things. It's all right of course—if anyone believed the truth, that the novel I have half finished is a very different matter, they'd publish the Sound of the River to give me a helping hand. Sad to say the facts are otherwise. No one does believe in me. That was all sound and fury or rather froth and bubble.

(Letter to Peggy Kirkaldy, 3 July 1946)

I have a book of short stories written during the war and just afterwards.

Constable did not want short stories and I never offered them to anybody else.

The Letters of Jean Rhys, selected and edited by Francis Wyndham and Diana Melly (New York: Elisabeth Sifton Books, Viking, 1984), 40, 43, 44, 167, 56, 99–100; 32, 60, 139, 171, 225, 244; 29, 171; 187, 190. Selection © Francis Wyndham and Diana Melly, 1984. Introduction copyright © Francis Wyndham, 1984. Letters copyright © the Estate of Jean Rhys, 1984. Reproduced by permission of Sheil Land Associates Limited and by permission of Penguin Books Ltd.

They are "dated" of course and perhaps *too* carefully written. A bit lifeless maybe. Nevertheless, I think there might be an idea or two knocking about. Especially in the last which is called "In September, Petronella." Dated. But purposely.

(Letter to Diana Athill, 11 June 1959)

I know Peggy that you don't care for Americans but they have one great virtue, they don't stifle criticism. You can write about the Chain Gang or a canned meat factory or a loony bin and what have you and there's a chance of an audience. But not here! The English clamp down on unpleasant facts and some of the facts they clamp down on are very unpleasant indeed, believe me.

(Letter to Peggy Kirkaldy, 4 October 1949)

I read a letter in the Observer last Sunday from some editor—Peter Green—promising to accept any story up to (of) the standard of "Boule de Suif." Well I should damned well think he would! And Hemingway's last thing. Why not add Prosper Merimée's "Carmen" for good measure.

Poor Boule de Suif. They won't let her rest—

The thing is I very much doubt whether any story seriously glorifying the prostitute and showing up not one but several British housewives to say nothing of two nuns!—their meannesses and cant and spite—would be accepted by the average editor or any editor.

And "La Maison Tellier"?—Well imagine—

Of course I may be quite wrong. I don't know much about it these days. But I do read a lot and have a very definite impression that "thought control" is on the way and ought to be resisted. But will it be resisted?

Why say as Mr Green does "I demand a positive and creative view of life?" What is that? And why *demand* a view of life. Not his business surely.

(Letter to Morchard Bishop, 27 January 1953)

Writing Habits, the Woman Writer

I think that the anglo-saxon idea that you can be rude with impunity to any female who has written a book is utterly *damnable*. You come and have a look out of curiosity and then allow the freak to see what you think of her. It's only done of course to the more or less unsuccessful and only by anglo saxons.

Well my dear if it were my last breath I'd say HELL TO IT and—to the people who do it—

(Letter to Evelyn Scott, 10 August 1936)

I know it seems stupid to fuss over a few lines or words, but I've never got over my longing for clarity, and a smooth firm foundation underneath the sound and the fury. I've learnt one generally gets this by cutting, or by very slight shifts and changes—

(Letter to Selma Vaz Dias, 9 November 1949)

It's fine—except that one cannot *feel* a rustle. One *hears* a rustle—and I don't think rustle is the right word for a man's dressing gown. I must have slipped up. Haven't got the MS either. Taffeta rustles and so do stiff silks I suppose, but wouldn't a man's dressing gown be a heavy silk? Please don't think me pernickety but every word must be exact. Like "The Daring young man on the Flying Trapeze," by Saroyan. Have you ever read it?

(Letter to Selma Vaz Dias, 12 November 1956)

I think I have had little success because I did not want it. Not in that way. Not really. Even now I cannot connect money or publicity with writing, though I adore money and need it badly, very. For me, these things are different—and opposed. Bitterly. I can only write for love as it were. I did once try to produce a story for the Saturday Evening Post for I was advised to do this. Well I made it all glitter and de luxe and so on but in the end I *could not stop myself* from letting the sad, mousey companion steal all the jewels and the lover too. And *get away* with this antisocial act. I did leave the lovely mondaine with other jewels, and the second best lover. But still! It doesn't do. I tore up this thing on which I'd spent months of anxious care, plus research, and have never tried again.

(Letter to Francis Wyndham, 14 September 1959)

No I never think of possible readers, only a few people can help—indeed I, well, have very mixed feelings about an audience, so I try to blot them out, do my best, alone or nearly. I've sometimes thought Maybe they feel this withdrawal. If so it can't be helped, for that is how I've always felt.

(Letter to Diana Athill, 26 June 1963)

She [Selma Vaz Dias] has been very kind to me, as you know, and I am fond of her. But, I think, she *forgets*—Also she thinks that writing is easy. I have told her that it is hard. Very hard. I have told her that it isn't a penny in the slot and I don't think she believes me.

There is no penny, no slot. Not thousands of pounds could work that slot if it existed. There is only trying to make something out of nothing, or what seems to be nothing. (Except of course disbelief in oneself and failure and emptiness. And above all waiting for the time when all that does not count).

(Letter to Francis Wyndham, 11 October 1963)

Dominica, West Indies

I'm awfully jealous of this place (as you gather no doubt) I can't imagine anybody writing about it, daring to, without loving it—or living here twenty years, or being born here. And anyway I don't want strangers to love it except very few whom I'd choose—most sentimental. (But they *are* a bit patronising you know.) However I've an idea that what with rain, cockroaches, and bad roads etc Dominica will protect itself from vulgar loves.

(Letter to Evelyn Scott, 1936)

When I say I write for love I mean there are two places for me. Paris (or what it was to me) and Dominica, a most lovely and melancholy place where I was born, not very attractive to tourists!

(Letter to Francis Wyndham, 14 September 1959)

Autobiography?

You know, I would like to send you a very short story and implore you to type it for me.

It is not (repeat *not*) autobiography, and not to be taken seriously. But the people here are terribly narrow minded and they gossip like crazy.

Really—this is true! I found it out in Bude I assure you. For them "I" is "I" and not a literary device. Every *word* is autobiography!

This thing is called *"They Thought it was Jazz"* and is quite short but I don't want to give it to a girl round here who is doing some stuff for me.

(Letter to Maryvonne Moerman, 22 June 1960)

Part 2

I've always hated personal publicity. (*Why Necessary?* Only the writing matters.) . . .

I used to think that all writing should be anonymous. Was I so far wrong? A bit unfair perhaps, to past strivings.

(Letter to Francis Wyndham, 21 July 1960)

David Plante's Conversations with Jean Rhys

She said, "Listen to me. I want to tell you something very important. All of writing is a huge lake. There are great rivers that feed the lake, like Tolstoy and Dostoevsky. And there are trickles, like Jean Rhys. All that matters is feeding the lake. I don't matter. The lake matters. You must keep feeding the lake. It is very important. Nothing else is important."

Tears came to my eyes.

"Do you believe that?" she asked.

"Yes."

"But you should now be taking from the lake before you can think of feeding it. You must dip your bucket in very deep."

I blinked to rid my eyes of tears.

She said, "I think and think for a sentence, and every sentence I think for is wrong, I know it. Then, all at once, the illuminating sentence comes to me. Everything clicks into place." . . .

I felt I could ask her anything. I said, "Do you ever think of the meaning of what you write?"

"No. No." She raised a hand. "You see, I'm a pen. I'm nothing but a pen."

"And do you imagine yourself in someone's hand?"

Tears came to her eyes. "Of course. Of course. It's only then that I know I'm writing well. It's only then that I know my writing is true. Not really true, not as fact. But true as writing. That's why I know the Bible is true. I know it's a translation of a translation of a translation, thousands of years old, but the writing is true, it *reads* true. Oh, to be able to write like that! But you can't do it. It's not up to you. You're

Excerpted from David Plante, *Difficult Women: A Memoir of Three* (London: Victor Gollancz, 1983), 22, 30–1, 34, 38, 52. Reproduced by permission of Aitken, Stone & Wylie Limited.

picked up like a pen, and when you're used up you're thrown away, ruthlessly, and someone else is picked up. You can be sure of that: someone else will be picked up. No one in England has been picked up in a long while, no one in Europe, no one in America—"

"In South America?"

The expression burst from her like a revelation. "Yes! Yes!" Then she paused. "Perhaps."

Jean often talked of the "shape" of her books: she imagined a shape, and everything that fit into the shape she put in, everything that didn't she left out, and she had left out a lot.

She raised her hands and dropped them. "Oh, that: writing. No nothing ever justifies what you have to do to write, to go on writing. But you do, you must, go on. You hear a voice that says, 'Write this,' and you must write it to stop the voice. I don't hear any voices any more. My last collection of stories was no good, no good, magazine stories. I wasted two and a half years on that book. Not good. Oh, the reviews say it's good. But you know when you've done something good, and those stories are no good. I can't do it any more."

"You know," she said, "I was just thinking about the differences in our writing. I can't make things up, I can't invent. I have no imagination. I can't invent character. I don't think I know what character is. I just write about what happened. Not that my books are entirely my life—but almost. You invent, don't you?"

I said, "I suppose I do."

I helped her to her chair across the room.

On the slow way, she said, "Though I guess the invention is in the writing. But then there are two ways of writing. One way is to try to write in an extraordinary way, the other in an ordinary way. Do you think it's possible to write in both ways?"

"No," I said.

"You understand?"

"I think so."

"I think what one should do is write in an ordinary way and make the writing seem extraordinary. One should write, too, about what is ordinary, and see the extraordinary behind it."

Part 3

THE CRITICS

Introduction

Rhys was never quite the pariah she could, on occasion, make herself out to be.[1] Despite the fact that she clearly felt herself to be a literary outcast for large parts of her career, one is struck both by her literary and publishing contacts even in very bleak periods of her life, and also by the generally very positive tenor of her reception in contemporary reviews.[2] The extracts from these reviews of *The Left Bank*, *Tigers Are Better-Looking*, and *Sleep It Off Lady* provide a representative selection of the perceptive and generally sympathetic commentary that these volumes received. Reviews of *The Left Bank*, when they go beyond mere summary and notice, provide some very astute commentary on the work. They also appear in very substantial reviewing journals. Conrad Aiken's review in the *New York Evening Post* remarks on the author's technical skill and her ability to present the essentials of any situation depicted. The company he places Rhys in—Katherine Mansfield, Ernest Hemingway—is also striking and very positive. The anonymous reviews in the *New Statesman* and the *Times Literary Supplement* are also thoroughly positive and lay out the terms in which much future Rhys criticism will operate—the unified world of her stories and the social and moral hostility of the author toward the powerful and well-heeled. Both U.S. and British reviews take their cue to some extent from Ford Madox Ford's Preface to *The Left Bank* (an extract of which is printed here), which, among other things, praises Rhys's technical skill (her "instinct for form") and her violent, "almost lurid" "passion for stating the case of the underdog."

The much later reviews of *Tigers Are Better-Looking* also emphasize Rhys's interest in the underdog and outsider. The reviewers in *Publishers Weekly* and in *The New Republic* set forth clearly the argument that the world of Rhys's short fiction is a unified one in which certain concerns and figures are recurrent. While several reviewers comment on the narrowness of the range of that world, Diane Johnson in the *Washington Post* argues for its universality—"this nether world is the demimonde where the human heart really lives." Commentators emphasize the bleakness of the author's vision of the world, marked above all by a sense of human exclusiveness and cruelty. The question of possible sentimentality and self-pity in that world is also raised and fruitfully discussed. Stylistic matters too receive commentary, for example, from George Stade in the *New York Times Book Review*, but the limited space at most reviewers' disposal means that such comments are often cursory. It is interesting to note Robert Leiter's comment in the *New Republic* that Rhys must be seen as an innovative writer in the early twentieth century; this placing of her in the context of literary modernism anticipates later academic criticism of Rhys.

Once again, reviews of *Sleep It Off Lady* are fundamentally positive. Susannah Clapp in the *New Statesman* touches upon many of the major themes of Rhys criticism—the "bleak treats" of her dark, unified vision of the world, her avoidance of sentimentality, and the pared down and astringent style. Nick Totton's review in the *Spectator* raises issues of style and also the vexed issue of the autobiographical elements in Rhys's fiction.

Rayner Heppenstall's essay on Rhys, "Bitter-sweet" from 1968, provides a useful bridge to more academic criticism, placing her, as it does, in the context of innovative early–twentieth-century writing, touching upon the issue of autobiography and pointing to the consistent world of her fiction. These are two of the three main themes in Jean Rhys criticism (with reference both to novels and short stories). The themes that pervade Rhys criticism are: the unified world of her fiction; the presence of concerns associated with race, class, and gender in that fiction, and the associated issue of the importance of exile and the West Indies for her writing; and the question of biographical/autobiographical elements within her literary output.

Paul Piazza's appreciation of Rhys in the *Chronicle of Higher Education* is quite representative of a critical approach which sees Rhys as, in essence, writing the same or at least a very similar story constantly throughout her career. Such a position underlies both the complex and academic criticism of Judith Kegan Gardiner and Coral Howells as well as the more superficial comments in essays on "the Rhys woman" and "the Rhys world." This can either be seen positively, as it is by Piazza and numerous other commentators, or rather negatively, as, for example, by Linda Bamber in the *Partisan Review*.

Many critics such as Gardiner, Mary Lou Emery, Veronica Marie Gregg, Molly Hite, Howells, Gayatri Chakravorti Spivak, and V. S. Naipaul have put forward very persuasive cases for seeing the West

Indian experience and that of the exile, which is so typically part of that experience, as central to Rhys's fiction. They have also argued strongly that Rhys is very much concerned in her writing to scrutinize issues connected with race, class, and gender, and that she must take her place as an astringent analyst of the processes whereby certain kinds of people, particularly women, are marginalized and destroyed by the power of wealth and language which lie in the hands of (usually) men. In this context it is worth pointing, however, to the powerful arguments of Linda Bamber, Linda Niesen de Abruna, and Gloria Fromm, who insist that Rhys's political, social, and gender analysis is rather feeble and limited, and that it is a travesty of her writing to make it the vehicle for social criticism of any but the most rudimentary kind. In Part 1 of this study, we argue that Rhys's depictions of the outsider are rooted in specific social, historical, and cultural situations, but dissenting voices are by no means to be dismissed out of hand.

The biographical underpinnings of Rhys's work form a final major concern of Rhys criticism. A view of Rhys's work as simply transposed autobiography is most clearly given in Carole Angier's *Jean Rhys: Life and Work* (1990), a work which, despite its lavish detail, must be seen as highly dubious in its seamless mixing of fact and fiction. Both Hite and Gregg (the latter at greater length in the article quoted below) have argued against this view of Rhys's writing. Our own argument is that, while Rhys certainly used material from her own life, that material is transformed and used for fictional purposes in her texts. To see her work as confession and therapy must be judged finally as demeaning, for it suggests that was all she, and by implication, perhaps, all women writers, could do.

The following section contains selections from a range of reviewers and critics of Jean Rhys's short fiction. The line between review and criticism is admittedly an artificial one, but it seems reasonable to present separately contemporary reviews, written shortly after a book's appearance, and more general essays or book-length studies written at greater distance from the works' publication dates. However, shared concerns and comments run through both contemporary reviews of Rhys's volumes of short stories and later critical studies. Occasionally we have also included extracts from essays which examine Rhys's work as a whole in cases where the comments seem illuminating with regard to the short fiction as well as to the novels.

Notes

1. Her letter to Evelyn Scott of 10 August 1936, or to Francis Wyndham of 14 September 1959, both of which are printed in the previous section, are representative (*Letters*, 32, 171).

2. Even when she was living in some poverty in the 1950s and 1960s, Rhys was able to place any stories she did have available in good journals. See, for example, her letter to Francis Wyndham of 14 September 1959, thanking him for his introduction to "Till September, Petronella," which had been accepted for publication in the *London Magazine*, along with "The Day They Burned the Books" and "Tigers Are Better-Looking."

Conrad Aiken　　Miss Rhys cut[s] down to essentials with a vengeance. She has found, or is finding—though one dare not predict of an artist whose style is still forming—a mode for herself which, in a sense, is a compromise between the modes of Katherine Mansfield and Mr. Ernest Hemingway. I don't mean to suggest that she has been influenced by either of these writers, or, at any rate, not in the least perceptibly. One story, it is true, in this book reminds me of Miss Mansfield—Vienne, which is like a Viennese version, with profound differences and delicious variations, of *Je ne parle pas Français*; the staccato, excited tone of this, its speed, its irony, its gayety, the exquisite lightness with which it glides over a tragic darkness, all these qualities just faintly suggest the Mansfield story. But in general there is no trace of influence. Miss Rhys is like Miss Mansfield simply in her passion for laying hold, instantly, of essentials. She wants to give you a character in a single scene, or a single small episode. And she does it. There is no nonsense about her—she goes right for her point. No rhetorical introduction, no wistful peroration; the bare facts of the case barely stated, almost indeed as if truculently admitted. Mr. Ford complains amusedly in his preface that he tried in vain to induce Miss Rhys to add, here and there, a few descriptive sentences or phrases— for the purpose of producing atmosphere; but Miss Rhys was firm on the point—was in fact, thereafter, more drastic in this regard than ever. And in this she is like Mr. Hemingway. Bare dialogue—here and there

Extracted from Conrad Aiken, Review of *The Left Bank* by Jean Rhys, *New York Evening Post*, 1 Oct. 1927, 10. "Stories Reduced to Essentials: Jean Rhys a Remarkable New Hand Disdains to Squander Any Phrases on Atmosphere" by Conrad Aiken. Originally appeared in *The Saturday Evening Post*. Copyright 1927 by Conrad Aiken. Reprinted by permission of Brandt & Brandt Lit. Agents, Inc.

a meager stage direction, with its "She looked out of the window," or "He smiled"—more often, the mere—"he said."

Anonymous Reviewer in the *New Statesman*   In a number of essays and sketches Miss Rhys pictures post-war life in the Latin Quarter of Paris. She writes with very considerable skill, exhibiting a microscopic exactitude in detail and a care for the precise epithet; her portraits are interesting, if not exhilarating. The sketches mostly are brief, some of two or three pages only. They are "slices of life"—and cross-sections at that—rather than stories; what generally happens in them is . . . that nothing happens. It is visiting day in a prison; the warder bullies an old man, but smiles and steps aside for a pretty girl. A young man, weary of all women, is seated upon a park bench; a girl with legs "not bad" passes him; he follows her. A poet is in despair, because of the weather; he reflects upon the number of days he has still to live—"It was the last straw. The poet paid for his drinks." This last would seem to be the characteristic gesture of the men and women inhabiting these pages. There is melodrama, tragedy even, here, but sophisticated beyond sympathy. Love, fame, life itself—they turn, one and all, upon the question of paying for drinks. To question the significance of such an attitude is not to belittle Miss Rhys's talent; if Mr. Ford's admiration, like too many of his admirations, is a little exaggerated, it is certainly not misplaced.

Anonymous Reviewer in the *Times Literary Supplement*   In his interesting preface Mr. Ford writes with easy authority about the particular qualities of Parisian Bohemianism, and his slightly consultatory air as of a specialist called in suddenly for an important diagnosis, is distinctly pleasing. By comparison, Miss Rhys's sketches and short character studies seem almost tentative. Miss Rhys has an intimate knowledge of the Rive Gauche, but she is inclined to disturb the necessary content of her work by a rather self-conscious antagonism towards the Anglo-American invaders of Paris and her championship of the outcast, un-

Extracted from Review of *The Left Bank and Other Stories* by Jean Rhys, *New Statesman*, 30 April 1927, 90. Copyright *New Statesman & Society*. Reproduced with kind permission of *New Statesman & Society*.
Extracted from Review of *The Left Bank and Other Stories* by Jean Rhys, *Times Literary Supplement*, 5 May 1927, 320. First published in the *Times Literary Supplement*. Reproduced by permission of the *Times Literary Supplement*.

happy and fallen. She attains joy in her quick objective sketches of mannequins, models and artists, and her glimpses of those English spinsters who are to be found, lonely and forgotten, in tiny niches of the Latin Quarter have pathos and insight. Her subjective studies, written in the French manner in the first person, are less effective; this sensitized style always seems to produce a contrary, amateurish effect in English. "La Grosse Fifi," a story of a good-hearted though mercenary woman on the Riviera, is the most sustained piece of writing in the book and it is the best; the rather sordid theme is lightened by complete humanity and humorous charity. This fine study proves that Miss Rhys requires space and a certain amount of plot-action to give free play to her original talent.

Ford Madox Ford   Setting aside for the moment the matter of her very remarkable technical gifts, I should like to call attention to her profound knowledge of the life of the Left Bank—of many of the Left Banks of the world. For something mournful—and certainly hard-up!—attaches to almost all uses of the word *left*. The left hand has not the cunning of the right: and every great city has its left bank. . . . And coming from the Antilles, with a terrifying insight and a terrific—an almost lurid!—passion for stating the case of the underdog, she has let her pen loose on the Left Banks of the Old World—on its gaols, its studios, its salons, its cafés, its criminals, its midinettes—with a bias of admiration for its midinettes and of sympathy for its law breakers. It is a note, a sympathy of which we do not have too much in Occidental literature with its perennial bias towards satisfaction with things as they are.

. . . What struck me on the technical side—which does not much interest the Anglo-Saxon reader, but which is almost the only thing that interests me—was the singular interest for form possessed by this young lady, an instinct for form being possessed by singularly few writers of English and by almost no English women writers. I say "instinct," for that is what it appears to me to be; these sketches begin exactly where they should and end exactly when their job is done. No doubt the almost exclusive reading of French writers of a recent, but not the most recent, date has helped.

Extracted from Ford Madox Ford, "Preface: Rive Gauche," *The Left Bank and Other Stories* by Jean Rhys (London: Jonathan Cape, 1927), 23–5. Used by permission of Janice Biala.

Francis Hope   This is not art which consoles, or explains, or even constructs anything beyond itself. This may explain why the end of "The Lotus" is such a failure; even death seems too positive. The women who litter these pages have no luck; they are not even equipped with the consolation prize of righteousness. The barrier between this writing and mere whining is paper-thin, but it is the best paper, and it holds. All it permits are moments of aesthetic intuition, like the song the West Indian woman hears in Holloway jail in "Let Them Call It Jazz"; but even these will be taken away and falsified by others. Miss Rhys, unlike her characters, can make more of them. She, and her readers, are lucky.

Anonymous Reviewer in *Publishers Weekly*   It is fascinating to see how the later work hones away girlishness, pares excess (not that there was much to start with) and description to leave a tough astringent prose, laced with off-hand humor. This brings to life Miss Rhys's characters—her beastly, powerful men, her wry-mouthed prudish matrons, and above all her girls. It is the girls one especially remembers. They are really aspects of the same anxious, feckless, hard-drinking, penniless girl, walking the tightrope between respectability and semi-sluttishness, trying erratically to keep at bay the bourgeois "timid tigers" who will attack her when she's down and out. ⟩

Diane Johnson   . . . she is the chronicler of the seedy, cold and cruel. It may seem at first reading that her range, though perfectly handled within its limits, is nonetheless a limited range. . . .

Yet there is a sense in which this nether world is the demimonde where the human heart really lives, and it is this which gives Rhys her power and her significance. Reading these stories is like touring a gallery of Impressionist paintings; we understand the messages in the eyes of the absinthe drinker, in the weary shoulders of the woman

Extract from Francis Hope, "Did You Once See Paris Plain?" Review of *Tigers Are Better-Looking* by Jean Rhys, *Observer*, 31 March 1968, 29. Francis Hope The Observer ©. Published by permission of The Observer ©.

Extracted from Review of *Tigers Are Better-Looking*. Reprinted from the August 26, 1974 issue of *Publishers Weekly*, published by R. R. Bowker Company, a Xerox company. Copyright © 1974 by Xerox Corporation.

Extracted from Diane Johnson, "Overdrawn at the Left Bank of the World," Review of *Tigers Are Better-Looking*, *Washington Post Book World*, 3 November 1974, 1. © 1974, The Washington Post. Reprinted with permission.

with the flatiron. Rhys is an Impressionist writer, getting her effects with phrases like vivid brushstrokes. The magnificent story "Outside the Machine," for example, might be a painting of a hospital ward in which the figures speak, and say all that need be said about cruelty, hope, pain, poverty, the search for oblivion.

In all her stories, a person is faced with the ruthless imperatives of society—the need for money first, and then for respectability.

Robert Leiter   Perhaps I have made this collection sound limited in scope and repetitious in manner. It is not. It is acidly humorous and more varied in technique than one would imagine. Jean Rhys has found new ways to tell her basic story. Much of what she first did in the '20s and '30s has become routine fare in present-day fiction, so that her works may not seem so remarkable to us now; a historical perspective is a prerequisite in evaluating this exceptional artist. The publication of *Tigers Are Better-Looking* will be an important part of this process.

George Stade   I do not like this heroine or the fiction in which she appears, although I probably should. The prose is sharp, rapid, without affectation, and there are moments of clammy fascination, moments when the author gets you to share her obsessions. Maybe I am becoming claustrophobic. Certainly the heroine's self-pity becomes annoying if only because her author does not see around it. There is no distinction whatsoever between the way the heroine sees herself, other people, her situation, and the way Jean Rhys sees them. The heroine's self-pity and self-absorption wash back over the image we form of the author. Just the same, it is good to have the fiction in which this heroine is reproduced with such loving fidelity. The proof of the fidelity is that after having read the fiction, you realize how often you have met its heroine and just why you wish you hadn't.

Extracted from Robert Leiter, Review of *Tigers Are Better-Looking, The New Republic,* 7 December 1974, 24. Reprinted by permission of *The New Republic,* © 1974, The New Republic, Inc.
Extracted from George Stade, "A Spark, an Amis, a Rhys," Review of *Tigers Are Better-Looking, New York Times Book Review,* 20 October 1974, 6. Copyright © 1974 by The New York Times Company. Reprinted by permission.

Susannah Clapp   The sixteen short stories in Jean Rhys's new collection investigate varieties of dislocation: ruin—moral and physical—in the West Indies: displacement and disenchantment in London and Paris during and between the wars: the shrivelling worlds inhabited by the old and lonely. They are coolly and barely told; never windy, often funny.

The Dominican stories come closest to moral fable. A child's life is jangled, first by the suicide of a benign eccentric, later by the sexy stories of an old man; a marriage is skewered by an unexpected scandal; a nun cheats exile from the island by dying. There is occasionally too strong a sense of Q.E.D. at the ending of these stories—where a woman formulates the notion that her husband is "a complete stranger," or a shocked child reassesses the future pattern of her life. The strangeness of the experiences themselves are sufficiently persuasive and stand in no need of prompting or conclusion. Miss Rhys's stories are often best when they are simply beautifully shaped slivers, which register not different experiences so much as possible attitudes and expressions. The London tales are particularly cunning in their pinning of style to observable ephemeral. A girl feels her own youth fade as vigour seeps from the outside world—in Britain the laundry van no longer calls, and in Germany the women "simply *slink* about"—and her wanness turns to hysteria when her flat-mate jollies herself up with "old girl."

At times Jean Rhys seems on the point of self-parody—in danger of writing essays on desertion in which abandoned hats in gutters and half-empty buses collude too easily with a heroine too gracefully wispy. But the wistfulness is always spiked with astringency—by a detachment of observation which accommodates both the seductive unscrupulousness of whores in flat barred shoes and skimpy tunics, and the cad, whose disappointment at failing to conquer is compounded by pique when the elegance of his smoking jacket goes unremarked. Most individual when her narrator is in the wings rather than in the centre, she is always capable of springing bleak treats.

Extracted from Susannah Clapp, "Bleak Treats," Review of *Sleep It Off Lady*, *New Statesman*, 22 October 1976, 568–8. Copyright *New Statesman & Society*. Reproduced with kind permission of *New Statesman & Society*.

Part 3

Nick Totton   *Sleep It Off Lady* is not so much a collection of short stories as a kind of autobiography. But autobiography must be a work of creation as well as of reconstruction: Jean Rhys treads the boundary between fiction (always with its sources in recollection) and history (always fictionalised by the pattern-seeking mind). She gives us a series of sharp, sudden images—some pieces are no more than a couple of pages long—which have been enriched through long immersion in that mysterious living element, the memory. . . .

Jean Rhys's style is so fine, so accurate, that one is scarcely aware of her having a style at all. She knows how to stand out of the way of her stories. In fact the themes presented here suggest that an ambivalent perception of invisibility has played a central role in her life. But whatever its place in Jean Rhys's history—and her own tact puts detective work to shame—it has contributed to a subtle and unique literary personality. What is offered here is, in a sense, what one person has learnt from a long and varied life: given not as homilies, but far more generously, still embodied in the events and people which were the occasion for learning. Some of the stories are substantial, formally organised and pointed; others are like the apparently irrelevant yet still demanding memories that are the real stuff of our lives.

Rayner Heppenstall   In those days, too, one heard of unjustly neglected writers, notably women. One who was frequently urged on me was Mary Butts. I did not hear of Jean Rhys. I read Mary Butts and liked what I read, though I felt that too much had been claimed for her. My reaction to Jean Rhys has been much the same, at least in respect of her earlier writings.

The pleasing thing about her rediscovery is that it rekindled her energies, so that she finished *The Wide Sargasso Sea* [sic]. Those energies were not, it is true, quite dormant. Half of the stories in the present volume were written after the outbreak of Churchill's war. But, just as I find *The Wide Sargasso Sea* more interesting than Miss Rhys's earlier novels, so, in the present volume, the story I most admired was "Let Them Call It Jazz," apparently the last written. A virtue shared by that novel and this story is that, although both draw on memories of a

Extracted from Nick Totton, "Speak Memory," Review of *Sleep It Off Lady*, *The Spectator*, 30 October 1976, 22. Reproduced by permission of *The Spectator*.
Extracted from Rayner Heppenstall, "Bitter-sweet," Review of *Tigers Are Better-Looking*, *The Spectator*, 5 April 1968, 446–7. Reproduced by permission of *The Spectator*.

West Indies childhood (and the story also on memories of dismal lodgings round Notting Hill), neither is at all directly autobiographical. Both required a detachment and an imaginative effort not always evident elsewhere.

The sketches from *The Left Bank*, first published in 1927, do not pretend to be anything more than that, were indeed originally subtitled "sketches and studies of present-day Bohemian Paris." "La Grosse Fifi" and "Vienne" are, no doubt, properly stories, but much of the rest is the merest *reportage*, though I don't suppose it was called that then. It is less than brilliant. *Pace* her most dedicated admirers, I don't think that sharpness either of eye or ear were ever Miss Rhys's most conspicuous gifts. In "Vienne" we seem already to be with that composite heroine who, under a variety of names, moves unhappily through the earlier novels, ditched by some man, bitched by other women, lost, drinking, broke, sometimes ill, sleeping on veronal and luminal, holding back tears or failing to hold them back.

The same figure reappears in the later stories, is called Petronella, Inez, Teresa, can hardly be Lotus quite, can hardly be Maidie, has no name, remembers Dominica, is commonly in England but once at a clinic in Versailles.

. . .

And yet for my money, or, indeed, without money, life to the very end of the decade remained pleasanter than it is now, and there seemed to be more good writers around. This, at any rate, will have to be my generation's excuse for ignoring Jean Rhys. It had nothing to do with Hitler, unemployment and Stephen Spender. They worried us, but not unduly.

Paul Piazza   All Rhys's novels and stories detail the downward spiral of the same woman, who appears under different names and at various stages. A child of the tropics, the Jean Rhys woman finds London cold and depressing, Paris hostile and mean. She possesses no resources, financial or otherwise, and thus no future. She is picked up, periodically kept as a mistress, abandoned and deceived by various men—men who are neither cruel nor coarse, merely indifferent. The

Extract from Paul Piazza, "The World of Jean Rhys," *The Chronicle of Higher Education*, 7 March 1977, 19. Reprinted by permission of Paul Piazza and *The Chronicle of Higher Education*.

Rhys woman is a female Prufrock, unable to "get on." "Life is cruel and horrible to unprotected people," complains Marya Zelli in *Quartet*.

One way to fight off the inevitable gloom is to purchase clothes, which the Jean Rhys woman does with desperate abandon. Grooming her hair and polishing her nails are also methods of asserting the self. Monica in "The Insect World" (a story from the new collection [*Sleep It Off, Lady*]) comments that the Nazis wisely removed nail polish from the market because once they've got a girl thinking she isn't pretty "they've got her where they want her, as a rule. And it might start with nail polish, see?" Endless streets of one-night cheap hotels, the longed-for oblivion of alcohol and sleep are for the Rhys woman last-ditch measures, preludes to darkness.

Jean Rhys's stories offer no answers, few questions: Life merely happens. A refrain in *Quartet*, "There she was," reads like a one-line biography of the Rhys heroine. At best, existence is a complicated, random affair of cafés, dingy rooms, shiftless men who sometimes pay, sometimes don't, dresses that will be lucky, dresses that won't. Unlike the Hemingway hero, the Rhys heroine can hone no code from her despair.

A summary of Jean Rhys's plots is inadequate, even depressing; yet reading the stories proves a surprisingly exhilarating experience. Cleansed of any excess, her style is near perfect: not a scene, not a word, is wasted. Through a line of dialogue or a mere sentence or two of description, Rhys compresses a life. The writing in this new collection is as swift and severe as strychnine.

Molly Hite　　Rhys does tell her own story, of course, and in this respect she resembles many other twentieth-century writers. But to make biography the principle that governs interpretation of her works is to make Rhys unable to control the form and ideology of her own text. There can be little question of innovation or even of technique, and no question of a deliberate challenge to the value presuppositions of the dominant culture, when criticism tries to naturalize the unsettling questions raised within a body of fiction by making them the effect

Extracted from Molly Hite, *The Other Side of the Story: Structures and Strategies of Contemporary Feminist Narrative* (Ithaca and London: Cornell University Press, 1989), 22, 24–5. Copyright © 1989 by Cornell University. Used by permission of the publisher, Cornell University Press.

of a constricted point of view that the author herself was unable to transcend.

Yet many readers find it difficult to call the situation of any of Jean Rhys's protagonists ordinary, at least in part because the problems involved in naming these characters tend to invoke weirder problems about what to *do* with them, deposited as they are in the foreground of narratives that chronicle only their incapacity to control their own lives. The question of what to do with them arises because the Rhys woman doesn't seem to do much for herself, or not anything that works, nothing that significantly improves her situation or even renders it tragic. She is often characterized as "passive" or "masochistic" because her actions do not substantially change her lot, as if she did not have the *efficacy* to be a protagonist. And readers like the student who resented paying attention to a "floozy" tend to feel that if she is going to be this sort of person she ought to get out of the way, out of the spotlight; she ought to fade back into the shadows at the periphery of the story where they won't have to look at her at all the time.

This last sort of reaction is valuable, precisely because it acknowledges how unsettling the Rhys woman is to dominant cultural presuppositions. Both mainstream and feminist critics who admire Rhys's fiction in effect try to settle her, accommodating her to these presuppositions either by interpreting her as an alien and inferior sort of person who serves as an object of study (in the process sacrificing authorial empathy), or by interpreting her as Rhys's own unexamined self-projection (in the process sacrificing authorial control). But such adjustments, made in order to justify the protagonist, take for granted that the protagonist requires justification. They begin from the presumption that she is the sort of character who, under normal circumstances would not be major, and then they redefine the circumstances without questioning the underlying premises: that there are intrinsically major and minor characters, regardless of narrative context, and that certain categories of socially marginal human beings are by virtue of this social marginality fitted only to be minor characters.

To articulate these premises is to allow Jean Rhys's achievement to be restated in terms of radical innovation. Rhys continually places a marginal character at the center of her fiction and in doing so decenters an inherited narrative structure and undermines the values informing this structure. In particular the novel, a form that emerged with the bourgeoisie and embodies the ethical priorities of this ascendant class, privileges agency—and, more insidiously, privileges the assumption that an agent who is motivated and tenacious enough will necessarily bring about the desired results.

Veronica Marie Gregg   The deliberate elimination of such elements [of setting] from her own work is based on Rhys's awareness of her difference from writers like Ford and his own literary models and precursors. Rhys's concern is as separate as she is from the dominant values which underpin the art and ideology of metropolitan society. She was in the metropolitan centres and appropriated the terms and theories which gave impulse to the artistic movements, but she was not of that world. As a woman and West Indian, she existed at the moral, aesthetic and hence ideological juncture of the metropolis. In imperial Europe, her home, the periphery, existed as a negation, an absence. Rhys herself was aware of this from the very beginning. When she was told that she would be introduced to Ford, who thought that some of the expatriate writers in Paris were very important, Rhys asked herself: "Am I an expatriate? Expatriate from where?"

Rhys's attention to the *mot juste*, her emendations, deletions and corrections, demonstrate that her simple sentences are achieved after careful attention to social detail, linguistic selection, literary tradition, and the sound and rhythm of the words themselves. The meaning of her work is processed by the form. Between the fourth and fifth drafts [of "Before the Deluge"] there are almost ninety corrections, deletions and transformations of sentences. Between the fifth and sixth, there are nine changes and ten deletions. Most of the corrections to the fifth draft include the deletion of descriptive words like "very" and "almost," the substitution of shorter phrases for long ones and the rearrangement of words in a sentence.

Laura Niesen de Abruna   Since the 1970s there has been a plethora of books and articles . . . that praise Rhys's fiction as feminist or social statement. Despite this, the evidence in the fiction itself, in her

Extracted from Veronica Marie Gregg, "Jean Rhys and Modernism: A Different Voice," *Jean Rhys Review* 1 (Spring 1987): 32, 40. Reproduced by permission of *Jean Rhys Review*. Extracted from Laura Niesen de Abruna, "Jean Rhys's Feminism: Theory against Practice," *World Literature Written in English* 28, no. 2 (1988), 327. Reprinted by permission of *World Literature Written in English*.

autobiography *Smile, Please*, and in the recently published letters shows that Rhys's "theories" about woman's place in society were anti-feminist. We know that when she read a review of her work that was evenly mildly feminist, she laughed and tore it up. . . . Often she seems hostile to other women; they are part of an unexamined and unexplained paranoia that pervades her fiction and autobiographical writings. Except in her last novel, Rhys's fictional women never seek a solution for their isolation in relationships with other women. Either the thought does not occur to them, or the women they meet are more ruthless, vicious and competitive than the men.

Linda Bamber   Notably absent from Rhys's account of her heroine is any analysis of her plight in political terms. The Rhys heroine is a natural victim, not a victim of sexual politics or class oppression. As an exile of obscure origins she is more or less classless; and although she certainly feels brutalized by men, she insists that "I'm even more afraid of women." The problem is extremely general: "People are such beasts, such mean beasts," says the heroine of *After Leaving Mr. Mackenzie*. Elsewhere the formula is simply "life is cruel and horrible to unprotected people." The social analysis of Rhys's work stops with the assertion that there are outsiders and insiders, and that the one is entitled to resent the other. But even the resentment is fitful and limp. The Rhys heroine knows that she is largely responsible for her own unhappiness. Whenever something good comes her way—money, a man, the possibility of a good time—she instantly loses it through laziness, obsessiveness, or a kind of petty anger arising from her sense that it isn't enough.

Nancy J. Leigh   To be a woman in Rhys's fiction is to be a victim; women are excluded from economic and emotional security, alienated from their bodies and sexuality and barred from power or independence by a society bent on creating female roles to meet male social and sexual needs. . . .

The mature protagonists in Rhys's novels—Marya Zelli, Julia Mar-

Extracted from Linda Bamber, "Jean Rhys," *Partisan Review* 49 (1982): 94. Reproduced by permission of Linda Bamber.
Extracted from Nancy J. Leigh, "Mirror, Mirror: The Development of Female Identity in Jean Rhys's Fiction," *World Literature Written in English* 25, no. 2 (1985), 271. Reprinted by permission of *World Literature Written in English*.

tin, and Sasha Jansen, as well as several women in the short stories—
so completely internalize the expectations (and limitations) masculine
society places on what it means to be female that they drift in aimless,
self-destructive passivity which leads only to continued poverty, sexual
exploitation and finally to complete breakdown. . . . Rhys is not, however, simply a chronicler of female victimization; she is also an acute
observer of the forces which shape women's identities and a stylist
capable of reflecting these observations in her use of language.

Coral Ann Howells   The double bind repeatedly rehearsed in her
[Rhys's] fictions is that despite their awareness of the social structures
within which they are trapped, her heroines do not attempt to break
out; instead they assiduously try to stay within the conditions of their
entrapment, where every new instance of betrayal represents another
expulsion from paradise. Though her fictions offer a merciless exposure
of a female predicament, women's resistence to the metanarrative of
male imperialism is undermined by their being caught in a "movement
between complicity and critique," as Rachel Blau Du Plessis describes
the dilemma of modernist women writers. These fictions do not offer
solutions to women's dilemmas, but they are radical investigations of
the social and psychological constructions of gender as Rhys writes in
suppressed female narratives which deconstruct ready-made definitions
of Woman in favour of representations of individual women. It is in this
invention of a dialogue situation that her fictions are so innovatory. . . .

Extracted from Coral Ann Howells, *Jean Rhys* (New York: St. Martin's Press, 1991), 13.
Copyright © 1991 by St. Martin's Press. First published by Harvester Wheatsheaf,
Hemel Hempstead, U.K., 1991. Reprinted by permission of Harvester Wheatsheaf and
St. Martin's Press, Incorporated.

Chronology

1890   Jean Rhys born (real name: Ella Gwendoline Rees Williams) in Roseau, Dominica, to Welsh father and Creole (i.e., of family long-settled in the West Indies) mother.

1907   Goes to England, attends Perse School for Girls (1907–9) and Academy of Dramatic Art (1909).

1919–1921   Lives at various times in Holland, Vienna, and Paris. Marries Jean Lenglet, a Dutch writer. A son dies in infancy, and a daughter, Maryvonne, is born.

1923   Meets Ford Madox Ford. Lenglet is imprisoned and then extradited to Holland for illegal entry into France and for breaking currency regulations.

1924   "Vienne" published under the name of Jean Rhys in Ford's *the transatlantic review*.

1927   *The Left Bank and Other Stories*, with a preface by Ford, is published by Jonathan Cape.

1928   *Postures* (*Quartet*) published by Chatto and Windus.

1930   *After Leaving Mr. Mackenzie* published by Jonathan Cape.

1933   Divorce from Jean Lenglet.

1934   Marries literary agent Leslie Tilden Smith. *Voyage in the Dark* published by Constable.

1936   Visits Caribbean (Martinique, St. Lucia, Dominica) and New York.

1939   *Good Morning, Midnight* published by Constable.

1939–1945   Lives in various provincial English towns and London. Her daughter Maryvonne and Lenglet are in Holland (occupied by Germans 1940–44). Leslie Tilden Smith dies (1945).

1947   Marries Max Hamer, a lawyer, cousin of Tilden Smith.

1948   Conflict with neighbors leads to assault charges. Rhys is

131

remanded in custody for a week in Holloway Prison. She answers Selma Vaz Dias's advertisement in the *New Statesman* inquiring of Rhys's whereabouts.

1950–1952 Hamer imprisoned for larceny.

1956 *Good Morning, Midnight* broadcast by the B.B.C.

1957 Receives a 25-pound advance from publishers André Deutsch for *Wide Sargasso Sea*.

1966 Hamer dies after lengthy illness. *Wide Sargasso Sea*, published by Deutsch, receives the Royal Society of Literature Award and the W. H. Smith Award. Rhys is made a Fellow of the Royal Society of Literature.

1968 *Tigers Are Better-Looking* (consisting of unpublished stories and of stories from *The Left Bank*) published by Deutsch.

1969 "I Spy a Stranger" and "Temps Perdi" published in *Penguin Modern Stories*.

1976 *Sleep It Off, Lady* published by Deutsch.

1978 Made a CBE (Commander of the Order of the British Empire).

1979 Dies. *Smile, Please*, a partial autobiography, published by Deutsch.

Selected Bibliography

Primary Works

Published Collections of Short Stories

My Day: Three Pieces. New York: Frank Hallman, 1975. "My Day," "Invitation to the Dance," "Close Season for the Old?"

Sleep It Off Lady. London: André Deutsch, 1976. "Pioneers, Oh, Pioneers," "Goodbye Marcus, Goodbye Rose," "The Bishop's Feast,""Heat," "Fishy Waters," "Overture and Beginners Please," "Before the Deluge," "On Not Shooting Sitting Birds," "Kikimora," "Night Out 1925," "The Chevalier of the Place Blanche," "The Insect World," "Rapunzel, Rapunzel," "Who knows What's up in the Attic?" "Sleep It Off Lady," "I Used to Live Here Once."

The Collected Short Stories. Introduction by Diana Athill. New York and London: Norton, 1987. "Illusion," "A Spiritualist," "From a French Prison," "In a Café," "Tout Montparnasse and a Lady," "Mannequin," "In the Luxemburg Gardens," "Tea with an Artist," "Trio," "Mixing Cocktails," "Again the Antilles," "Hunger," "Discourse of a Lady Standing a Dinner to a Down-and-out Friend," "A Night," "In the Rue de L'Arriveé," "Learning to Be a Mother," "The Blue Bird," "The Grey Day," "The Sidi," "At the Villa d'Or," "La Grosse Fifi," "Vienne," "Till September Petronella," "The Day They Burned the Books," "Let Them Call It Jazz," "Tigers Are Better-Looking," "Outside the Machine," "The Lotus," "A Solid House," "The Sound of the River," "I Spy a Stranger," "Temps Perdi," "Pioneers, Oh, Pioneers," "Goodbye Marcus, Goodbye Rose," "The Bishop's Feast," "Heat," "Fishy Waters," "Overture and Beginners Please," "Before the Deluge," "On Not Shooting Sitting Birds," "Kikimora," "Night Out 1925," "The Chevalier of the Place Blanche," "The Insect World," "Rapunzel, Rapunzel," "Who Knows What's up in the Attic?" "Sleep It Off Lady," "I Used to Live Here Once," "Kismet," "The Whistling Bird," "Invitation to the Dance."

The Left Bank and Other Stories. Preface by Ford Madox Ford. London: Jonathan Cape, 1927. "Illusion," "A Spiritualist," "From a French Prison," "In a Café," "Tout Montparnasse and a Lady," "Mannequin," "In the Luxemburg Gardens," "Tea with an Artist," "Trio," "Mixing Cocktails," "Again the Antilles," "Hunger," "Discourse of a Lady Standing a Dinner to a

Down-and-out Friend," "A Night," "In the Rue de L'Arriveé," "Learning to Be a Mother," "The Blue Bird," "The Grey Day," "The Sidi," "At the Villa d'Or," "La Grosse Fifi," "Vienne."
Tigers Are Better-Looking with a Selection from The Left Bank. London: André Deutsch, 1968. *Tigers Are Better-Looking*: "Till September Petronella," "The Day They Burned the Books," "Let Them Call It Jazz," "Tigers Are Better-Looking," "Outside the Machine," "The Lotus," "A Solid House," "The Sound of the River." *The Left Bank*: Preface by Ford Madox Ford, "Illusion," "From a French Prison," "Mannequin," "Tea with an Artist," "Mixing Cocktails," "Again the Antilles," "Hunger," "La Grosse Fifi," "Vienne."

Uncollected Stories

"The Christmas Presents of Mynheer Van Rooz." *Time and Tide*, 28 November 1931, 1360–61.
"The Joey Blagstock Smile." *New Statesman*, 7 September 1974, 23–30; December 1977, 890.
"Vienne." *the transatlantic review*, December 1924, 639–45. (This consists of sections later used in the version of "Vienne" printed in *The Left Bank*.)

Other Works

Novels
After Leaving Mr. Mackenzie. London: Jonathan Cape, 1931.
Good Morning, Midnight. London: Constable, 1939.
Postures. London: Chatto and Windus, 1928. (U.S. edition: *Quartet*. New York: Simon & Schuster, 1929.)
Voyage in the Dark. London: Constable, 1934.
Wide Sargasso Sea. London: André Deutsch, 1966.

Poetry and Essay
"Four Poems: 'Night on the River,' 'All Through the Night,' 'A Field Where Sheep Were Feeding," and 'To Toni'." *Observer*, 20 February 1977, 30.
"Q and A: Making Bricks without Straw." *Harper's*, July 1978, 70–1.

Translations
Barred by Edouard de Nève. Translated by Jean Rhys. London: Desmond Harmsworth, 1932. (De Nève was a pseudonym of Rhys's first husband, Jean Lenglet.)
Perversity by Francis Carco. Translated by Ford Madox Ford. Chicago: Pascal Covici, 1928. (Jean Rhys translated this novel, not Ford.)

Nonfiction

Smile, Please: An Unfinished Autobiography. Foreword by Diana Athill. London: André Deutsch, 1979.

Letters

Letters, 1931–1966. Selected and edited by Francis Wyndham and Diana Melly. London: André Deutsch, 1984.

Secondary Sources

Interviews

Cantwell, Mary. "A Conversation with Jean Rhys." 1974. In *Critical Perspectives on Jean Rhys*, ed. Pierrette Frickey, 21–7. Washington, D.C.: Three Continents Press, 1990.
Plante, David. *Difficult Women: A Memoir of Three.* London: Victor Gollancz, 1983.
Vreeland, Elizabeth. "Jean Rhys: The Art of Fiction LXIV." *Paris Review* 21, no. 76 (Fall 1979): 218–37.

Books

Angier, Carole. *Jean Rhys: Life and Work.* Boston, Toronto, and London: Little, Brown and Company, 1990.
Dash, Cheryl M. L. "Jean Rhys." In *West Indian Literature*, ed. Bruce King, 196–209. London: Macmillan; Hamden, Conn.: Archon Books, 1979.
Davidson, Arnold E. *Jean Rhys.* New York: Frederick Ungar, 1985.
Emery, Mary Lou. *Jean Rhys at "World's End": Novels of Colonial and Social Exile.* Austin: University of Texas Press, 1990.
Gardiner, Judith Kegan. "The Exhilaration of Exile: Rhys, Stead, and Lessing." In *Women's Writing in Exile*, ed. Mary Lynn Broe and Angela Ingram, 134–50. Chapel Hill: University of North Carolina Press, 1989.
———. *Rhys, Stead, Lessing, and the Politics of Empathy.* Bloomington and Indianapolis: Indiana University Press, 1989.
Gregg, Veronica Marie. "Jean Rhys on Herself as a Writer." In *Caribbean Women Writers: Essays from the First International Conference*, ed. Selwyn R. Cudjoe, 109–115. Wellesley: Calaloux, 1990.
Hite, Molly. *The Other Side of the Story: Structures and Strategies of Contemporary Feminist Narrative.* Ithaca and London: Cornell University Press, 1989.
Howells, Coral Ann. *Jean Rhys.* New York: St. Martin's Press, 1991.

James, Louis. *Jean Rhys*. Critical Studies of Caribbean Writers. London: Long-
man, 1978.

le Gallez, Paula. *The Rhys Woman*. New York: St. Martin's Press, 1990.

Morrell, A. C. "The World of Jean Rhys's Short Stories." In *Critical Perspectives
on Jean Rhys*, ed. Pierrette Frickey, 95–102. Washington, D.C.: Three
Continents Press, 1990.

Sage, Lorna. *Women in the House of Fiction: Post-War Women Novelists*. New
York: Routledge, 1992.

Staley, Thomas F. *Jean Rhys: A Critical Study*. Austin: University of Texas
Press, 1974.

Wolfe, Peter. *Jean Rhys*. Twayne's English Authors Series. Boston: Twayne
Publishers, 1980.

Articles and Reviews

General

Alvarez, A. "The Best Living English Novelist." *New York Times Book Review*,
17 March 1974, 6–7.

Bailey, Paul. "Bedrooms in Hell." Review of *Quartet* and *After Leaving Mr.
Mackenzie*, *Observer*, 18 May 1969, 30.

Bamber, Linda."Jean Rhys." *Partisan Review* 49 (1982): 92–100.

Braybrooke, Neville. "The Return of Jean Rhys." *Caribbean Quarterly* 16,
no. 4 (1970): 43–6.

Brown, Nancy Hemond. "England and the English in the Works of Jean
Rhys." *Jean Rhys Review* 1 (Spring 1987): 8–20.

Casey, Nancy J. "The 'Liberated' Woman in Jean Rhys's Later Short Fiction."
Revista Interamericana Review 4 (Summer 1974): 264–72.

de Abruna, Laura Niesen. "Jean Rhys's Feminism: Theory against Practice."
World Literature Written in English 28, no. 2 (1988): 326–36.

Fromm, Gloria. "Making up Jean Rhys." *New Criterion*, December 1985,
47–50.

Jordis, Christine. "Jean Rhys ou la perspective de l'exil" (Jean Rhys or the
Perspective of Exile). *La Nouvelle Revue Francaise* (July–August 1983):
156–67.

Leigh, Nancy J. "Mirror, Mirror: The Development of Female Identity in
Jean Rhys's Fiction." *World Literature Written in English* 25, no. 2 (1985):
270–85.

Lindroth, James R. "Arrangements in Silver and Grey: The Whistlerian Moment in the Short Fiction of Jean Rhys." *Review of Contemporary Fiction*
5, no. 2 (1984): 128–34.

Morrell, A. C. "The World of Jean Rhys's Short Stories." *World Literature
Written in English* 18, no. 1 (1979): 235–44.

Naipaul, V. S. "Without a Dog's Chance." Review of *After Leaving Mr. Macken-zie*, *New York Review of Books*, 18 May 1972, 29–31.

Richardson, Dorothy. "Utterly Other Discourse: The Anticanon of Experimental Women Writers from Dorothy Richardson to Christine Brook Rose." *Modern Fiction Studies* 34 (1988): 437–47.

Spivak, Gayatri Chakravorty. "Three Women's Texts and a Critique of Imperialism." *Critical Inquiry* 12 (Autumn 1985): 243–61.

The Left Bank and Other Stories

Aiken, Conrad. "Stories Reduced to Essentials." *New York Evening Post*, 1 October 1927, 10.

"A Mistress of the Conte." *New York Herald Tribune Books*, 6 November 1927, 16.

Ford, Ford Madox. "Preface: Rive Gauche." *The Left Bank and Other Stories* by Jean Rhys. London: Jonathan Cape: 7–27.

"Miss Rhys's Short Stories." *New York Times Book Review*, 11 December 1927, 28, 30.

Nation and Athenaeum, 25 June 1929, 424.

New Republic, 16 November 1927, 345.

New Statesman, 30 April 1927, 90.

Saturday Review of Literature, 5 November 1927, 287.

Spectator, 30 April 1927, 772.

Times Literary Supplement, 5 May 1927, 320.

Thompson, Irene. "The Left Bank Apéritifs of Jean Rhys and Ernest Hemingway." *Georgia Review* 35 (Spring 1981): 94–106.

Wyndham-Lewis, D. B. "Hinterland of Bohemia." *Saturday Review*, 23 April 1927, 637.

Tigers Are Better-Looking

Angier, Carole. "Weekend in Gloucestershire: Jean Rhys, Adrian Allison and 'Till September Petronella'." *Jean Rhys Review* 4, no. 1 (1990): 2–14.

Bailey, Paul. Review of *Tigers Are Better-Looking*. *London Magazine*, June 1968, 110–111.

Baker, Roger. "Brief and Potent." *Books and Bookmen*, June 1968, 34–5.

Brown, Nancy Hemond. "Aspects of the Short Story: A Comparison of Jean Rhys's 'The Sound of the River' with Ernest Hemingway's 'Hills Like White Elephants'." *Jean Rhys Review* 1 (Fall 1986): 2–12.

Byatt, A. S. "Trapped." *New Statesman*, 29 March 1968, 421–22.

Haltrecht, Montague. "More from Jean Rhys." *Sunday Times*, 24 March 1968, 52.

Heppenstall, Rayner. "Bitter-sweet." *Spectator*, 5 April 1968, 446–7.

Hope, Francis. "Did You Once See Paris Plain?" *Observer*, 31 March 1968, 29.

Selected Bibliography

Jebb, Julian. "Sensitive Survivors." *Times*, 30 March 1968, 21.
Johnson, Diane. "Overdrawn at the Left Bank of the World." *Washington Post Book World*, 3 November 1974:1–2.
Leiter, Robert. Review of *Tigers Are Better-Looking*. *New Republic*, 7 December 1974, 22–4.
"Losing Battles." *Times Literary Supplement*, 2 May 1968, 466.
Moss, Howard. "Going to Pieces." *New Yorker*, 16 December 1974, 161–64.
Review of *Tigers Are Better-Looking*. *Publishers Weekly*, 26 August 1974, 299.
Review of *Tigers Are Better-Looking*. *Library Journal*, 15 November 1974, 2983.
Stade, George, "A Spark, an Amis, a Rhys." *New York Times Book Review*, 20 October 1974, 4–6.
Suarez, Isabel Carrera, and Esther Alvarez Lopez. "Social and Personal Selves: Race, Gender and Otherness in Rhys's 'Let Them Call It Jazz' and *Wide Sargasso Sea*." *Dutch Quarterly Review of Anglo-American Letters* 20 (1990–92): 154–62.
Sullivan, Mary. "All Underdogs." *Listener*, 25 April 1968, 549.
Sullivan, Walter. "The Short Story Again." *Sewanee Review* 83 (July–September 1975): 537–46 (539–40).
Tyler, Ralph. "Luckless Heroines, Swinish Men." *Atlantic* 235 (January 1975): 81–4.
Wilson, Lucy. " 'Women Must Have Spunks': Jean Rhys's West Indian Outcasts." *Modern Fiction Studies* 32 (Autumn 1986): 439–47.

Sleep It Off Lady
Auchinloss, Eve. "Lighting up the Inner Dark." *Washington Post Book World*, 7 November 1976, G1–2.
Bailey, Paul. "True Romance." *Times Literary Supplement* 22 October 1976, 1321.
Bell, Pearl K. "Letter from London." *New Leader*, 6 December 1976, 3–5.
"Briefly Noted." *New Yorker*, 10 January 1977, 98.
Clapp, Susannah. "Bleak Treats." *New Statesman*, 22 October 1976, 568–9.
Crane, Peggy. "Writers in an Alien Land." *Books and Bookmen*, February 1977, 60–61.
Gould, Tony. "In a Dark Wood." *New Society*, 28 October 1976, 209.
Harcourt, Joan. *Queen's Quarterly* 84 (1977): 512–13.
Heidenry, John. *Commonweal*, 30 September 1977, 632, 634.
Macauley, Robie. "Things Unsaid and Said Too Often." *New York Times Book Review*, 21 November 1976, 7, 50.
Mellors, John. "World Shrinkers." *Listener*, 22 and 30 December 1976, 854.
Pollitt, Katha. "Books in Brief." *Saturday Review*, 13 November 1976, 40–1.
Review of *Sleep It Off Lady*. *Publishers Weekly*, 27 September 1976, 74.
Totton, Nick. "Speak Memory." *Spectator*, 30 October 1976, 22.

Tyler, Anne. "Boundaries and Bonds: Concerning Strangers in Strange Lands." *National Observer*, 11 December 1976, 18.

Wilmers, Mary-Kay. "Some Must Cry." *New Review*, November 1976, 51–2.

Wood, Michael. "Endangered Species." *New York Review of Books*, 11 November 1976, 30–33.

Bibliographies

Frickey, Pierrette M., ed. *Critical Perspectives on Jean Rhys*. Washington: Three Continents Press, 1990. (This contains a very useful bibliography.)

Gaines, Nora. Bibliography. *Jean Rhys Review* 3 (Fall 1988): 14–20.

Jacobs, Fred Rue. *Jean Rhys: Bibliography*. Keene: The Loop Press, 1978.

Mellown, Elgin W. *Jean Rhys: A Descriptive and Annotated Bibliography of Works and Criticism*. New York and London: Garland, 1984.

Index

Index

"Grey Day, The": narrators and narration in, 3, 6; plot and action of, 12
"Grosse Fifi, La," 27–35, 50; circular patterning in, 17; critics on, 120, 125; ease of language in, 21; heroine in, 25; narrators and narration in, 3, 4, 6; plot and action of, 12; style of, 8, 9

"Heat," 7
Heath, Lotus (character, "The Lotus"), 22
Hemingway, Ernest, 115, 118
Heppenstall, Rayner, 116, 124–25
Hite, Molly, 116, 126–28
Hope, Francis, 121
Howells, Coral Ann, 104, 116, 130
Hudson, Mrs. (character, "I Spy a Stranger"), 10, 12
"Hunger," 41; narrators and narration in, 5, 6; plot and action of, 11

"I Spy a Stranger," 64–71, 83, 88; gossip in, 86; narrators and narration in, 7; plot and action of, 12; protagonist in, 30; setting of, 13; style of, 10–11
"I Used to Live Here Once": narrators and narration in, 7; setting of, 13
"Illusion," 15–20, 89; heroine in, 22; narrators and narration in, 3, 4, 5, 6; "outsider" characters in, 18; plot and action of, 12; setting of, 13; style of, 8
"Imperial Road," 19
"In a Café," 4, 5
"In the Luxembourg Gardens," 3
"In the Rue de l'Arrivée": narrators and narration in, 5, 6; style of, 9
"Insect World, The": critics on, 126; plot and action of, 11, 12; style of, 10
"Invitation to the Dance," 7

Jeffries, Walter (character, *Voyage in the Dark*), 39
Johnson, Diane, 115, 121–22
Julian (character, "Till September Petronella"), 36, 37

Kipling, Rudyard, 11, 81
Kirkaldy, Peggy, 105, 106, 107
"Kismet," 3, 7

Laboriau, Madame (character, "Learning to Be a Mother"), 34–35
Laura (character, "I Spy a Stranger"), 10, 12, 64–71, 86
"Learning to Be a Mother": compassion in, 34–35; happiness and motherhood in, 23; heroine in, 25; limits to happiness in, 27; narrators and narration in, 6; "outsider" characters in, 18, 26; plot and action of, 12; style of, 8, 9
Left Bank, The, 15, 27; critics on, 115, 125; Ford's preface to, 5, 115, 120; narrators and narration in, 3–6, 7; plot and action of, 11–12; style of, 8–11
Leigh, Nancy J., 129–30
Leiter, Robert, 122
Lenglet, Jean, 105
"Let Them Call It Jazz," 42–46, 47, 48, 50, 51; colors in, 16; critics on, 121, 124; gossip in, 64; heroine in, 29, 30; limits to happiness in, 27; narrators and narration in, 3, 7; outsider status in, 74; plot and action of, 12; protagonist in, 14, 42–43; setting of, 13; style of, 11
Longa, Jimmy (character, "Fishy Waters"), 86, 87
"Lotus, The," 45; critics on, 121; heroine in, 21

"Mannequin," 20–27, 37, 63; narrators and narration in, 4, 6;

The Authors

Cheryl Alexander Malcolm took her B.A. at Emmanuel College, Boston, and her M.A. at the University of Warwick in England. She has taught at Tsuda College in Japan, the University of Gdańsk in Poland, and Olivet College in Michigan. Her poetry and translations have been published in Britain, Poland, and the United States. From 1994 to 1995 she was the recipient of a Fulbright Scholar award to Poland. She teaches American literature and culture at the University of Gdańsk.

David Malcolm took his M.A. at the University of Aberdeen, Scotland, and his Ph.D. at University College, London. He has taught at Wroxton College of Fairleigh Dickinson University, the University of Tokyo, the University of Gdańsk, and Olivet College, Michigan. His essays on British, German, and Polish literature have appeared in European and U.S. journals, and he has published numerous translations from Polish. He is Professor of English Literature and Culture at the University of Gdańsk.

The Editor

General editor Gordon Weaver earned his B.A. in English at the University of Wisconsin-Milwaukee in 1961; his M.A. in English at the University of Illinois, where he studied as a Woodrow Wilson Fellow, in 1962; and his Ph.D. in English and creative writing at the University of Denver in 1970. He is author of several novels, including *Count a Lonely Cadence*, *Give Him a Stone*, *Circling Byzantium*, and most recently *The Eight Corners of the World* (1988). Many of his numerous short stories are collected in *The Entombed Man of Thule*, *Such Waltzing Was not Easy*, *Getting Serious*, *Morality Play*, *A World Quite Round*, and *Men Who Would Be Good* (1991). Recognition of his fiction includes the St. Lawrence Award for Fiction (1973), two National Endowment for the Arts Fellowships (1974, 1989), and the O. Henry First Prize (1979). He edited *The American Short Story, 1945–1980: A Critical History*, and is currently editor of *Cimarron Review*. He is professor of English at Oklahoma State University. Married, and the father of three daughters, he lives in Stillwater, Oklahoma.